# THE FACTS OF DEATH

*For Paul*
*who died at six,*
*the safest year of life.*

# THE FACTS OF DEATH

Tony McCarthy

BELGRAVE PUBLICATIONS

First published in 2006 by
Belgrave Publications
Belgrave Avenue
Cork, Ireland
www.belgravepublications.com


Copyright © 2006 Tony McCarthy

A CIP record for this title is available from
The British Library.


ISBN 10:  0-9554376-0-1
ISBN 13:  978-0-9554376-0-1

# Contents

# Illustrations

# Acknowledgments

The research for this book was carried out in the last six months of 2005 and the first six months of 2006. Much of the material was accessed *via* the internet: scientific papers, articles from medical journals, news items, statistical compilations, books on a variety of topics, on-line medical dictionaries, encyclopaedias and other background material. Information was gathered from more websites than could possibly be acknowledged, so a general and sincere thanks is extended to all who have contributed to that wonderful resource.

I would like to thank my family for their support while I was writing and researching the book. My wife Angela, sons Steven and John, and daughter Mary Claire will, no doubt, be relieved that the topic of death will no longer be cropping up with such regularity at mealtimes. Steven also read the manuscript and offered some very useful suggestions.

Special thanks to Maurice Thuillier who obligingly read each chapter as soon as it was completed, and promptly returned an annotated version. Thanks also to Tim Cadogan, Noel Carroll and Finbarr O'Donovan for their valuable advice. The help of Dr Frances Lennon and Fr Michael Carroll in reviewing some technical details is gratefully acknowledged.

For everything there is a season
And a time for every matter under heaven:
A time to be born, and a time to die...
[ ECCLESIASTES 3: 1-2]


Oh death, where is thy sting-a-ling-a-ling
Or grave thy victory?
[1914-18 BRITISH ARMY MARCHING SONG
QUOTED IN BRENDAN BEHAN'S PLAY *THE HOSTAGE*]

# Introduction

Since your death is a certainty, you might consider it prudent to find out a little bit about that important topic. This book is a practical guide to death. While it does not intend to be ghoulish, it pulls no punches.

Denial is a common response to death. Chapter 1 examines some data relevant to this head-in-the-sand approach to mortality, and should put you in a more receptive frame of mind. Chapter 2 suggests how to work out the details of your own demise. You don't need to be a clairvoyant to find out what you're going to die from and when. Insurance companies routinely make such calculations on your behalf.

Chapter 3 examines one of the main fears of death: does it hurt? Modern medical science is providing more and more people with advanced warning of their deaths. When the bad news is given, that person is said to be 'dying'. This terminal stage of existence is looked at in Chapter 4. The prospect of being mistakenly pronounced dead and subsequently buried alive was an ancient fear. Chapter 5 examines the extent to which it may have occurred in the past and asks can such mistakes still be made. It looks in particular at new concepts of death, and organ donation. Important aspects of the funeral are dealt with in Chapter 6.

One writer put the two major problems raised by death rather succinctly. He compared the human being to a nut: the body is the outer shell, the soul or consciousness is the edible kernel. The practical and philosophical issues raised by the questions 'what will we do with the shell?' and, 'where is the nut gone?' comprise the material for the next two chapters. Chapter 7: 'After Death' takes a detailed look at the processes that the body undergoes in the grave. In recent years, due to the popularity of books and TV dramas on forensic medicine, people have become less squeamish about these matters. Chapter 8: 'Afterlife', gives brief descriptions of the afterlife, based on accounts from sacred texts and the teachings of various churches. This section includes new evidence that supports the idea of continued existence after death.

After all of that, it's time to make your 'death list': an inventory of important items that require attention, before it is too late. Chapter 9 suggests items that should be included in everybody's final 'to do' inventory.

The book ends with the chapter entitled, 'Last Words', which is a compilation of the final phrases spoken by some of the famous and infamous.

# 1. Denial

The prospect of annihilation is frightening. First, you imagine it as a permanent dreamless sleep, unconsciousness for ever and ever. Then you realise that the concept is more comprehensive than that. Annihilation means that there is no longer anything of you, even to be asleep or unconscious. Your state of being is as it was before your birth — non-existent. You no longer survive as an entity. You are gone.

The alternative to obliteration can be terrifying: rebirth in a strange world; a new bodiless state of being, perhaps in the hell described so graphically by the major religions. Add to that all the attendant horrors of human demise — the pain, the burial and putrefaction of the body — and it is easy to understand why the classic reaction to death is denial.

## Denial No. 1: A Very Ripe Old Age

The simplest denial of all is that death is not going to happen for a long, long time and, therefore, is best forgotten about. We allow ourselves to be assured that advances in medicine have conquered most diseases and that cures for the more intractable ones, like cancer, are just round the corner. That still leaves old age to be reckoned with, but the news from that final frontier has been positive since the 1960s. At that time, the medical world began to study longevity seriously. Researchers made their way to several remote areas noted for the long lifespans of the local people: places where the inhabitants were said to routinely live to be over 100 years and where several were reputed to have survived up to 140 years. A few were believed to have reached the incredible age of 150. Perhaps by copying their diet or imitating other aspects of their lifestyles, we too could stretch our lives into triple digits.

## GEORGIA

The most spectacular claims centred on communities in the Caucasus mountains, formerly part of the USSR, but now forming part of the independent states of Georgia, Armenia and Azerbaijan. A *National Geographic* article of January 1973 referred to a woman from the region who claimed to be over 130 years old. Furthermore, she took a shot of vodka each morning and smoked a pack of cigarettes every day! A census taken in 1970 indicated that in the Abkhazia region of Georgia, a much higher percentage of the population were aged 100 years or over, compared to populations in the highly developed countries of the West.

After studying the people of this region extensively, a Russian geneticist named Zhores Medvedev found that many of the supposed centenarians had actually assumed the identity of their dead parents and grandparents. One of the oldest centenarians appeared in a government newspaper on his 128th birthday, only to be unmasked as a fraud a few days later. It was discovered that he was one of the many World War I deserters who had been using his father's papers to avoid being found out. He was actually 78. Generally, these old stories tended to go unchallenged because the Soviet dictator Josef Stalin was a Georgian and he enjoyed tales of extraordinary old age from his native place.

Ultimately, due to the utter isolation of the region, poor record keeping and consistent confusion and lying about ages and identities, the notion that these mountain people lived to extreme old age was determined to be nothing more than a fantastic myth.

## VILCABAMBA

The Vilcabamba Indians of the Ecuadorean Andes were also put under the longevity microscope. Unfortunately, initial media reports of their exceptional longevity were based on no other evidence than the statements of the people themselves, with little or no backup from documentary sources. When one researcher returned to the area four years after his first visit, he found that one Miguel Carpio who, at the age of 121, had previously been the oldest man in the valley, had aged by 11 years in that four year period.

Radiologist Richard Mazess and anthropologist Sylvia Forman travelled to Vilcabamba to determine whether or not there was any validity to the claims of remarkable old age in the region. They carried out a house to house census and checked records of births, deaths and marriages, insofar as they existed, and cross checked various documents against each other. They found a pattern of age exaggeration and inconsistencies throughout the records. They discovered, for example, that Miguel Carpio, who had previously transformed from 121 to 132 in four years, was really 61 when he reported that he was 70. Five years later he claimed to be 80, and when he was really 87 he said he was 121. His mother was born five years *after* his own stated birth date.

Mazess and Forman concluded: 'Systematic age exaggeration was found after age 70 in an Equadorian population noted for extreme longevity. Extreme ages (over 100 years) were either incorrect or unsubstantiated. There was no evidence of increased longevity in the Vilcabamba population.'

THE HUNZA VALLEY
Claims of longevity among the people of the Hunza Valley in Kashmir were published in several books throughout the twentieth century. However, due to the lack of birth, marriage and death records, researchers had no means of ascertaining the ages of people apart from simply asking them. The Hunzas have no written documentation to corroborate evidence of age. Clearly, reports that the Hunzas have many more centenarians among them than other cultures, are simply anecdotal.

The 'long lived cultures' have several things in common. They are all located in remote villages with poor literacy skills where record keeping is patchy at best and often non existent. In their communities, age is considered to be honourable and extreme old age a state meriting reverence. Clearly, there is much to be gained from 'exaggeration'. Occasionally, there is also an economic benefit. The local governor of Vilcabamba referred to its ancient citizens as the areas 'oil wells', a reference to the much appreciated tourism which their fame attracted. Though their claims have long been discredited, the Vilcabamba website still refers to the area as 'The Valley of Long Life'.

## Denial No. 2: We Can Become Immortal

Looked at from space, the earth is a little speck. Coming closer, its spherical shape is revealed. Zooming in further, the continents and individual countries take shape. Closer again and towns, then streets can be seen, with crowds of people milling about. Focus on one individual person and continue with the ultra magnification and the incredible structure of the human body is revealed. It is composed of a galaxy of cells, thousands of billions of semi-independent repositories of life.

CELLS

Cells are the smallest structures capable of life processes, that is of taking in nutrients, expelling waste products and reproducing. They are the building blocks of all living things. They were first described in 1665 by the English scientist Robert Hooke. Looking at a piece of cork through a microscope of his own manufacture, he fancied that the tiny box-shaped structures, revealed by magnification, resembled the cramped living quarters of medieval monks — cells. The name stuck.

Some life forms, such as bacteria, consist of a single cell. Most organisms are composed of multiple cells. The human body has an estimated 20 to 30 trillion (add twelve zeros). Nobody has ever actually counted the number of cells in the body of a mature human being and some experts put the number as high as 100 trillion. It is not surprising, therefore, that, though human cells vary in size, all of them are microscopic. A selection of ten thousand would fit on the head of a pin.

Each individual cell is a separate living entity. The dozens of different types of human cells: skin, muscle, bone, etc, are organised into specialist groups called tissues. Different tissue types are assembled into organs, which in turn are combined to form body systems such as the circulatory, nervous and digestive systems, each carrying out a specialised function.

Every human being begins as a two-cell combination when a sperm cell fuses with an ovum. In order to grow and develop, these cells must be augmented, and in a fully grown human, the damaged or worn out cells must be replaced on a continuous basis. The manufacture of more cells, both for development and repair, is accomplished by cell division. This complex operation, called *mitosis*, results in the production of two genetically identical cells from a single cell. Biology books often simplify the process by the use of diagrams showing the 'O' shaped cell becoming pinched in the middle and gradually acquiring the shape of the number '8', and then becoming two O's. It is estimated that every second, 25 million cells are manufactured in the human body, simply to replace those that have finished their life cycle and died off.

Within the nucleus of a cell lies the DNA which embodies the master plan, not only for that particular cell, but also for the whole organism. A wide variety of cells may be created from the same DNA because genes, which provide cells with their unique characteristics, may be switched on or off.

PROBLEMS

Hopes of immortality depend on a quantum leap forward in the science of biology. Scientists must develop a clear understanding of cells: how they work and particularly how and why they malfunction. They must find a way of eliminating cancer cells, which develop in all bodies over time; find a way of counteracting the cumulative cell damage caused by aging; and find a way of ensuring that cells do not stop replicating themselves after they have divided a certain number of times. This is likely to require many decades of work because an individual cell is an incredibly complex structure. Each atom of its composition has an essential part in the overall design. The entire human body, combining countless cells in different formations, is immeasurably intricate.

DEATH IS BUILT IN

Scientists often use the Latin term *in vitro*, literally 'in glass', to describe a biological process made to occur outside the body in an artificial environment. *In vitro* fertilisation has been a topic of controversy for some years. *In vitro* human cell production has been going on for decades. Up to the 1960s scientists thought that human cells were immortal; that there was no limit to the number of times each succeeding generation could split into two identical copies of the mother cell. The fact that cell reproduction within the body tapers off with old age was thought to be the result of some overall controlling mechanism within the body.

This view was changed by the experimental work of American scientist Dr Leonard Hayflick. He discovered that there was a limit to the number of times a cell could divide. He claimed that after 50 to 80 divisions (depending on the cell type), cells became incapable of further division. So revolutionary were his findings that the *Journal of Experimental Medicine* to which he first submitted his scientific paper refused to publish it. The article was returned with the comment: 'The largest fact to have come from tissue culture in the past 50 years is that cells inherently capable of multiplying will do so indefinitely if supplied with the right milieu *in vitro*.' The paper was published later in the journal *Experimental Cell Research*. It has been cited in other scientific papers over 3,000 times since. Hayflick's experiments were repeated by others and his findings confirmed. The scientific community now accepts the finite nature of cell division. It is known as 'the Hayflick limit'.

In the decades which followed Hayflick's discovery, the mechanism that determines the number of duplications a cell is capable of undergoing was discovered. When a cell splits in two, the DNA double helix unzips itself and each half attracts the appropriate atoms and molecules to replace the half that has pulled away, forming two where once there was one. However, in the process, the ends of the DNA strands, called telomeres (tea-low-meer), shorten with each duplication. In this way, there is a crucial physical difference between a so called 'mother' cell and the two 'daughter' cells into which it splits. With each succeeding generation of cells, telomeres become progressively shorter. When the telomeres become too short, cells lose their capacity to divide.

The only exception to the Hayflick limit are cancer cells and reproductive cells. All other cells in the body will die off after a limited number of divisions. Theoretically, if you live long enough, all of the cells from which your body is composed will eventually die. The fact that death is literally built in to every cell in the body provides a huge challenge to the technology of immortality.

It has been discovered that the capacity of reproductive cells to divide in an immortal fashion, is due to the presence of a protein called telomerase, which prevents the shortening of telomeres. Researchers are working on the possibilities of introducing telomerase into normal cells to endow them with immortality.

CANCER

Telomerase is also very relevant to one of the greatest killers of modern times: cancer. Its presence in the makeup of cancer cells allows them to divide an unlimited number of times. Typically, cancer begins with a single rogue cell. Its uncontrolled division produces a malignant tumour. Cells from this lethal mass can break away, enter the blood stream and lymphatic system and lodge in other parts of the body, seeding secondary tumours.

The longer you live, the more likely you are to contract cancer. Immortality or the significant extension of human life cannot be accomplished without the eradication of this disease.

OLD AGE

Overcoming the problems presented by the Hayflick limit and surviving cancer and all other diseases, still leaves those who want to live forever with the problem of counteracting the symptoms of old age. Many theories have been advanced to explain why a person who has gone 'over the hill' begins to suffer simultaneously from thinning bones, weakening muscles, deteriorating immunity system and overall physical decline, which progresses unto death. A theory first published in the 1950s has gained widespread acceptance among researchers. It suggests that 'free radicals' are the chief cause of aging. Like their namesakes in the political world, free radicals subject the body to continuous attack; indeed, the oxygen atom, which is the chief culprit, could be described as a very subversive element.

A free radical is an atom or molecule that has one unpaired electron. As a result it is highly unstable and reactive. It will seek to acquire an electron from any available source. It may either steal an electron from another atom or molecule, or alternatively it may attach itself to another molecule sharing rather than acquiring another electron. This kind of activity inside a cell can be very damaging. If the free radical steals an electron, the molecule from which it acquired the electron, in turn, becomes a free radical and seeks to win an electron back from another source, thus starting a chain reaction. If it shares an electron, it attaches itself to another molecule, changing the makeup and properties of the molecule and possibly sabotaging some important cell function.

The part of a cell that produces energy, the mitochondria, turns out large numbers of free radicals as by-products of its processes, so these damage-causing particles are always present in big numbers within cells. It has been estimated that oxygen radicals damage the DNA inside each cell some 10,000 times per day. When a cell that has sustained DNA damage replicates itself, the new cells inherit the damage and pass it on in turn. Succeeding generations of cells sustain additional damage which they too transmit. Accumulated defects can reduce the efficiency of cells or cause them to malfunction.

The mortality of the cell, the unconquered diseases, the relentless attacks of free radicals are huge barriers to the prospect of immortality or even an extended life span. Despite this, many researchers are optimistic that dramatic increases in longevity are just round the corner. Their hopes are based on promises of a whole new area of study: nanoscience.

## NANOSCIENCE AND NANOTECHNOLOGY

Nano derives from 'nanus' the Latin word for dwarf. It means one billionth of something: a nanometre is one billionth part of a metre, a nanosecond is a billionth of a second. It is the measurement used in the world of atoms and molecules. Ten hydrogen atoms beaded together in a row would extend to about one nanometre. The width of a DNA molecule is about 2.5 nanometres. A human cell is thousands of nanometres in diameter.

The objective of nanotechnologists is to gain unprecedented control of the material world; to use the periodic table of elements as a catalogue of building materials, and to manufacture items atom by atom, virtually clicking them together as if they were part of a child's construction kit. Why use such tiny building blocks? A diamond and a lump of coal are both composed of carbon. The qualities of each are determined by the manner in which the individual atoms are arranged. The power to place carbon atoms in the formation that creates diamonds would allow the nanotechnologists to make diamonds from coal.

Take three little tanks of gas: oxygen, hydrogen and nitrogen; a little pile of carbon, calcium and salt; a few pinches of sulphur, phosphorus, iron and magnesium; and microscopic piles of twenty or so other elements — you have the ingredients of a human being. Nature, with its own version of nanoengineering, is able to convert these cheap and plentiful elements into a conscious, mobile, self-replicating, self-repairing creature. Nanotechnologists want to imitate nature's way of making things, atom by atom.

The first person to point to a future of extreme miniaturisation was Nobel prize-winner Richard Feynman in a lecture given in 1959 titled 'There is Plenty of Room at the Bottom'. Before personal computers or CD-ROMs had been invented, Feynman was able to show that it was theoretically possible to write all 25,000 pages of *Encyclopaedia Britannica* on the head of a pin. His ideas on miniaturisation were based on the possibility of being able to manipulate atoms individually, placing them exactly where they were wanted.

A little over 30 years later, in 1990, a headline grabbing demonstration showed the world that manipulation of individual atoms was not a dream. IBM scientists experimenting with an element called xenon – a gas often used in the headlights of cars to produce a blue light – managed to place 35 individual atoms so precisely that they spelled out the letters 'IBM'.

In 1986 K. Eric Drexler published *Engines of Creation* in which he sketched out the astounding changes that nanotechnology would bring about. Drexler dismisses the world of micro-electronics, currently the greatest area of miniaturisation in human manufacture, as fundamentally no different from the technology used by Stone Age people to fashion arrowheads. They hammered and chipped rocks composed of trillions of atoms until they attained the desired shape; computer chips are made by carving slices of silicon, also consisting of trillions of atoms. Drexler foresees a future in which 'assemblers', nano-sized machines, will assemble molecular structures. They will be able to bond atoms together in virtually any stable pattern, adding a few at a time until a complex structure is complete. It would take thousands of years for a single assembler to manufacture an item one atom at a time, so the first assembler project would be to make trillions of copies of themselves. Countless swarms of little workers would compensate for the tiny individual output. Eventually all manufacture would be carried out by these microscopic machines.

Drexler fired the imagination of many of his readers. Nanotechnology visionaries foresee: paint that can instantly configure to imitate its surroundings — for military use; bricks and other building materials that can sense weather conditions and then respond by altering their inner structures to be more or less permeable to air and humidity; paper-thin televisions; microwave-sized molecular manufacturing machines capable of manufacturing any item you want — one in every home.

Extreme miniaturisation, enabled by construction at atomic level, would revolutionise medicine. Computer controlled nanorobots, small enough to be injected into the bloodstream by the million, could intervene at a cellular and even molecular level, lengthening telomeres, fixing the damage done by free radicals, preventing and reversing the symptoms of old age. Cancer cells could be hunted down and destroyed.

In 2001, Nobel Prize-winner Richard Smalley, director of the Center for Nanoscale Science and Technology at Rice University in Houston, asked the question: 'Am I living in the last generation to die of cancer or the first generation to be saved by nanotechnology.' For Smalley it was a very poignant question. He was undergoing traditional cancer treatment and described chemotherapy as being 'hosed by almost lethal drugs…being taken next to death and then brought back again.' He described the procedure as the use of 'very coarse, brutal weapons.' The cure for cancer and all other diseases, he said will involve taking trillions of little nano-objects that will freely roam the body, distinguish cancer cells from healthy ones, and then kill the diseased cells. Crucially he added that such cures are still many years away.

Some scientists spurn the idea of human immortality, believing that the mission entrusted to the individual by nature, a mission programmed into every cell of our being, is to reproduce and raise offspring, then step aside and allow them to do the same — a mission completed in about 40 years. The immortality we need to protect, according to this way of thinking, is the immortal line of the germ cells that migrate from body to body down through the centuries, producing the eggs and sperm. As relay runners in the human race we become irrelevant after we've run our allotted course. Perhaps we should just enjoy passing on the baton, because despite the yearning of the human heart and breathtaking advancements in science, it looks like death is still inevitable for our generation.

# Denial No. 3: The Cryonics Lifeboat

If technology develops along the lines suggested by the nanodreamers, in fifty to a hundred years' time, people may be facing into lifespans of a thousand years and more. We may be within touching distance of immortality. If this is so, how tragic to be numbered among the last generations for whom life is short and death is inevitable.

Some people see a way out of this tantalising situation. It is called cryonics. Put briefly, cryonics involves the rapid freezing of the human body immediately after death in the hope of restoring it to life in the future. Until a cure for the disease that led to death is found, the body remains suspended in liquid nitrogen which prevents decay and further deterioration. The body storage capsules are like lifeboats carrying the hopeful forward to a time of miraculous technologies.

Cryology does not involve raising people from the dead. Supporters of the procedure point out that cardio-pulmonary resuscitation (CPR) brings clinically dead people back to life every day of the week. Prior to the development of the technique in the 1950s, people whose heart and lungs had stopped functioning would have been considered beyond human help. CPR can revive people who have been clinically dead for several minutes — in rare cases for several hours; cryology attempts to do no more than extend the period further, increasing it to years, perhaps centuries.

It is easy to dismiss cryology as a crackpot idea, and many commentators have poured scorn on it, however, its enthusiasts have advanced arguments which cannot easily be dismissed. Though no human being has been frozen and returned to life, human embryos have. John Brooks was removed from his mother's womb and suspended in liquid nitrogen for two months, after which he was carefully thawed, placed back in his mother's womb, and emerged — eleven months after being conceived — a completely healthy and normal child. Thousands of embryos have been successfully frozen since. Indeed, in one case, a human embryo was frozen in liquid nitrogen for a period of seven years and then brought to term, and is now a healthy child.

Many other biological specimens have been frozen, stored in liquid nitrogen and revived; these include whole insects, vinegar eels and many types of human tissue, including brain tissue.

In the 1970s, the technology to freeze and preserve human embryos was available, though it was not possible at that time to revive and transplant them to the womb. However, had embryos been preserved at that time, it would have been possible — a mere 10 years later — to thaw them out, transplant them in the womb and bring them to full term.

Cryology's main drawback at the moment is that freezing techniques currently in use cause major damage to human tissue. The formation of ice crystals in the super cooling process is the main culprit. Despite the use of anti-freeze agents called cryoprotectants, the problem has not been eliminated. Efforts are now being made to vitrify the body, that is, to cause it to harden in the same way that glass solidifies, without the formation of any crystals. Until this problem has been overcome, cryologists will continue to depend on future technologies, not only to cure the disease from which the patient died, but also to cure the damage caused by freezing.

If an animal, even as small as a mouse, could be vitrified and then revived, it would give cryology a credibility which it now lacks. Then, people would have the confidence to believe in the viability of freezing and reviving bigger animals and eventually even humans.

Once it can be demonstrated that freezing a human being is a reversible process, another major problem for the cryology lobby will be solved. Currently, a human being has to be certified as being dead before he or she can be legally frozen. Subjecting a person to a process that results in death, no matter what the stated intention, is regarded as homicide. This means that a patient who is suffering from a terminal disease must wait until the sickness has ravaged his body and killed him before he can be frozen and preserved for future medical treatment. This rather puts it up to future technologies. If freezing can be demonstrated to be reversible, a patient could opt to be frozen long before a terminal illness has caused too much damage, without the prospect of the cryologist facing a charge of homicide.

It may very well be the case that human life can be put on hold, stopped and restarted, as cryologists believe, and perhaps freezing or vitrification is the way to achieve this. However, time may show the methods currently in use to be unscientific. Before the invention of CPR, there was a long history of methods used, some ludicrous, to try to revive victims of drowning. They included flagellation — to try to stimulate some kind of response, and hanging the victim by the feet. According to *The New Zealand Medical Journal*, in 1767 the Dutch Humane Society published guidelines for resuscitation of victims of drowning, which included 'insufflation of smoke of burning tobacco into the rectum'. Time may show cryology, as currently practised, to be the technological equivalent of a puff of smoke up the exhaust pipe.

CRYOLOGY SERVICES

Robert Ettinger's book, *The Prospect of Immortality*, published in 1962, is credited with starting off the cryology movement. In the years after that, several groups were formed to discuss and eventually carry out the freezing and long term storage of human bodies.

One of the largest and the fastest growing of these organisations is the US-based Cryonics Institute (CI). Currently, CI have more than fifty bodies suspended in liquid nitrogen at a temperature of minus 196 degrees Celsius. The ages range from the mid-twenties to 100 years. A once-off payment to CI of $35,000 covers both the cost of the initial freezing and the annual maintenance charges.

Considering that the storage of bodies is for an indefinite period, CI's prices seem very low. Indeed, they are substantially lower than those of other providers, all of which charge fees in

FIGURE 1: CRYOSTATS FOR LONG-TERM CRYOGENIC STORAGE.

the region of $150,000. CI can charge less because it is a volunteer organisation with no paid staff. Also, its freezing techniques are low cost and CI relies more heavily on the ability of future technologies to repair freeze damage than organisations that use more advanced freezing techniques which limit freeze damage.

Some cryonics groups – but not the Cryonics Institute – offer the 'neuro' option. This involves freezing the head alone and disposing of the body. This cuts down considerably on the price tag of the service: a 'neuro' will cost $50,000. However, it requires the resurrection men of the future to literally put an old head on young shoulders. They will have to create a new body, reconnect the head, and repair the damage due to freezing — as well as curing the disease from which the person died.

Factors other than cost must also be taken into account by those considering crypreservation. The body must be prepared as soon as possible after death in order to minimise damage. The procedure involves an initial cool down with use of anticoagulant, removing the blood and replacing it with cryoprotectant. This is followed by further cooling and the long term immersion in liquid nitrogen at a temperature of minus 196 degrees Celsius. All of this takes place instead of the reposing in an open coffin at a funeral home and the funeral itself.

Much of this would not be to the liking of relatives. Unless they have been well prepared beforehand they may try to prevent cryopreservation going ahead. The neuro option is even more distressing. It must be rather difficult to have to go to the husband/wife or children of someone who has just passed away and to tell them that you are about to cut the head off the loved one, freeze it and place it in a tank with a dozen others.

The bargain basement of cryology involves burial in the Arctic permafrost. Some funeral homes in Canada and Alaska are willing to make such burial arrangements. Cryologists have little confidence in the revival prospects of such people.

Celebrities are now getting in on the act. The body of Ted Williams, the famous American baseball player who died on 5 July 2002, was flown to the Alcor Life Extension Foundation in Scottsdale, Arizona. His head was severed by surgeons and placed in a steel can filled with liquid nitrogen. His body stands upright in a 9 foot tall cylindrical steel tank, also filled with liquid nitrogen. His family split over the matter, a son and daughter approving of it and another daughter taking legal action to have the body released for cremation.

Even if future technologies give humans the capacity to bring back to life the cryopreserved, why would the people of the future want do so? Certainly, there would be a scientific value in doing it — once; and perhaps a novelty value in being able to converse with someone from the distant past. However, the notion that a society of the future would expend vast resources on thawing out people from the past is difficult to believe. A frozen specimen from a previous age, would be without any resources while requiring all kinds of advanced medical treatment.

In September 1991 two hikers discovered a frozen body high in the mountains between Austria and Italy. Detailed examination revealed it to be the body of a man in his 40s, but the body was estimated to be 5,300 years old, the oldest frozen mummy ever found. He became a world-wide sensation. The press dubbed him 'Ötzi the Iceman' after the Ötztal area where he was found. If it were possible to revive Ötzi what would become of him? After a round of TV chat shows and, perhaps, an appearance on *Celebrity Big Brother*, could he be expected to settle down happily in the twenty-first century? Would our generation be willing to thaw out, revive and look after an army of icemen? Would any generation?

# 2. Your Death: when and how

The longest lived person in the world, whose claim can be convincingly validated, was the Frenchwoman Madame Jeanne Louise Calment. She was born on 21 February 1875 and died on 4 August 1997 at the age of 122 years. Second in the longevity stakes was a Japanese man named Shigechiyo Izumi who is reputed to have reached the age of 120 years when he died in 1986. Some doubt has been cast on this claim by Dr John Wilmoth who discovered information to suggest that Izumi assumed the identity of an older brother and was 105 years old when he died. Less than thirty people have been reliably documented as surviving beyond the age of 110. The 'super centenarians' as they are called establish the upper limits of human survival at around 120 years. It is interesting to note that chapter 6, verse 3 of the *Book of Genesis* seems to promise that exact lifespan: 'Then the Lord said, "My spirit shall not abide in man forever, for he is flesh, but his days shall be a hundred and twenty years"'.

Many experts believe that maximum human lifespan is fixed and that increasing life expectancy is a result of the control and elimination of factors that led to early death. So, even though more and more people will reach the upper limits of human survival, the maximum human lifespan is unlikely to change. Optimistic commentators foresee a future in which cures for cancer, heart disease and other conditions will ensure that only in exceptional cases will a person die before living to the full potential of the human body; that death will be postponed until the body is literally worn out at the age of 120.

Disease, unhealthy lifestyles and poor living conditions still ensure that most of humanity die long before their time. Until people routinely live to 120, determining your death day, death year or even your death decade will continue to be difficult. However, a large body of statistical information should help you to make an informed estimate, and also to guess your cause of death.

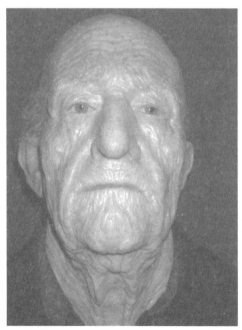

FIGURE 2: MASK OF DUSTAN HOFFMAN AS LITTLE BIG MAN: THIS MASK, ON DISPLAY IN THE A M E R I C A N MUSEUM OF THE MOVING IMAGE, NEW YORK, HELPED TO GIVE HOFFMAN THE APPEARANCE OF A 106 YEAR OLD MAN IN THE FILM *LITTLE BIG MAN* (1970). (PHOTO BY ALBERT FRIED-CASSORLA).

## *National Mortality Figures*

Lists of famous people, such as great artists, Nobel Prize winners, Presidents of the United States, etc, normally show the dates of birth and death in brackets after each name. If someone on the list is still alive, a little hyphen is placed after the date of birth with enough space left to insert the year of death: Bill Clinton (1946-   ). It is as if the pen is poised and the writer impatient to write in the terminal date.

In fact, there is a whole bureaucracy waiting to compile and process, not only the terminal dates of the famous, but numerous details about all deaths. Various officials are charged with recording this information. Normally, a doctor in attendance at a death fills out a Medical Certificate of Cause of Death, provided the death was due solely to some disease, that is, to natural causes. In most jurisdictions, non-natural deaths — which would include those resulting from accident, homicide and suicide — require officials other than a doctor, to carry out an investigation before registration. In Ireland, an independent official called a 'coroner' has legal responsibility for the investigation of sudden, unexplained, violent and unnatural deaths. In Scotland, the corresponding official is the 'procurator fiscal' who is involved in the certification of all sudden, suspicious, accidental, unexplained and unexpected deaths and any death occurring in circumstances that would give rise to serious public concern. In the US, investigations into suspicious deaths are carried out by a coroner, a medical examiner or a justice of the peace. Non-natural deaths may not normally be registered without a post mortem or an inquest or both. However, once all the extra paperwork has been completed, data concerning non-natural deaths are finally registered in the same way as deaths that did not arouse suspicion.

The World Health Organisation, from which most countries take the lead in matters pertaining to the registration of death, recommends a two-part death certificate. The first part is for recording the condition or sequence of conditions leading directly to death. There is room in this section for an immediate cause, one or more intermediate causes and an underlying cause of death. The underlying cause of death is literally the bottom line in a death certificate. It is defined as the disease or condition that initiated the train of events leading directly to death — in the case of a natural death; or the circumstances of the accident or violence which produced the fatal injury — in the case of non-natural deaths. Part II of a death certificate is for detailing any associated conditions which contributed to the death, but were not part of the causal sequence.

For example, a patient who dies a few hours after suffering a heart attack would have the medical term for this condition 'acute myocardial infarction' written into the topmost line of his death certificate as the immediate cause of death. However, his doctor would be expected to record any known condition that gave rise to the heart attack, such as 'atherosclerotic coronary vascular disease'. If this 'hardening of the arteries' was known to have been caused by another ailment, such as diabetes mellitus, that fact would also be included. Diabetes would be regarded as the underlying cause that initiated the train of events leading to death, even though it may have been contracted more than twenty years beforehand. The death certificate also requires the doctor to state the interval of time between the onset of the condition and the death of the patient. Thus, Part I of the certificate for the above patient would read: 'Acute myocardial infarction (12 hours), due to Atherosclerotic coronary vascular disease (3 years), due to Diabetes mellitus (25 years)'. Additional factors which contributed to the death, such as smoking and obesity, would be written into Part II of the certificate.

At the end of each year, all the national death data are sent to a country's central statistics office where they are used to compile annual mortality statistics. For these purposes, the most important details recorded on a death certificate are: the underlying cause of death, the age at death and, of course, the date of death so that it can be included in the statistics of the appropriate year.

INTERNATIONAL CLASSIFICATION OF DISEASES
The World Health Organisation (WHO) has standardised, in virtually all countries throughout the world, the way in which mortality statistics are compiled and published. The main tool used to accomplish this task is a document called the *International Statistical Classification of Diseases and Related Health Problems*, also known as the *International Classification of Diseases*, or simply as the *ICD*. It provides the essential ground rules for the initial certification and the subsequent coding and classification of cause of death data. It was developed collaboratively between the WHO and ten international centres. Countries are required to use the ICD under an agreement with the World Health Organisation that has the force of an international treaty. The ICD has been revised approximately every ten years to stay abreast of advances in medical science and to ensure the international comparability of health statistics. The tenth and most recent revision, ICD-10, replaced ICD-9 in the United States in 1999 and in Britain in 2001.

For the purposes of producing national mortality figures, the ICD divides all causes of death into 22 general categories, also called chapters, as follows:

| I | A00-B99 | Certain infectious and parasitic diseases |
|---|---------|-------------------------------------------|
| **II** | **C00-D48** | **Neoplasms (cancer)** |
| III | E00-E90 | Diseases of the blood and blood-forming organs and certain disorders involving the immune mechanism |
| IV | E00-E90 | Endocrine, nutritional and metabolic diseases |
| V | F00-F99 | Mental and behavioural disorders |
| VI | G00-G99 | Diseases of the nervous system |

| VII | H00-H59 | Diseases of the eye and adnexa |
|------|---------|--------------------------------|
| VIII | H60-H95 | Diseases of the ear and mastoid process |
| IX | I00-I99 | Diseases of the circulatory system |
| X | J00-J99 | Diseases of the respiratory system |
| XI | K00-K93 | Diseases of the digestive system |
| XII | L00-L99 | Diseases of the skin and subcutaneous tissue |
| XIII | M00-M99 | Diseases of the musculoskeletal system and connective tissue |
| XIV | N00-N99 | Diseases of the genitourinary system |
| XV | O00-O99 | Pregnancy, childbirth and the puerperium |
| XVI | P00-P96 | Certain conditions originating in the perinatal period |
| XVII | Q00-Q99 | Congenital malformations, deformations and chromosomal abnormalities |
| XVIII | R00-R99 | Symptoms, signs and abnormal clinical and laboratory findings, not elsewhere classified |
| XIX | S00-T98 | Injury, poisoning and certain other consequences of external causes |
| XX | V01-Y98 | External causes of morbidity and mortality |
| XXI | Z00-Z99 | Factors influencing health status and contact with health services |
| XXII | U00-U99 | Codes for special purposes |

Each of the 22 chapters is further divided into more specific categories. The subsections of Chapter II, 'Neoplasms' (the chapter name is printed in bold lettering in the above list for purposes of clarity) refer to the locations, on the human body, of the various types of cancerous tumours. The full list of 'Neoplasm' sub-sections is as follows:

## II C00-D48 Neoplasms (cancer)

| C00-C14 | Lip, oral cavity and pharynx |
|---------|------------------------------|
| C15-C26 | Digestive organs |
| C30-C39 | Respiratory and intrathoracic organs |
| C40-C41 | Bone and articular cartilage |

| | |
|---|---|
| **C43-C44** | **Skin** |
| C45-C49 | Mesothelial and soft tissue |
| C50 | Breast |
| C51-C58 | Female genital organs |
| C60-C63 | Male genital organs |
| C64-C68 | Urinary tract |
| C69-C72 | Eye, brain and other parts of central nervous system |
| C73-C75 | Thyroid and other endocrine glands |
| C76-C80 | Malignant neoplasms of ill-defined, secondary and unspecified sites |
| C81-C96 | Malignant neoplasms, stated or presumed to be primary, of lymphoid, haematopoietic and related tissue |
| C97 | Malignant neoplasms of independent (primary) multiple sites |
| D00-D09 | In situ neoplasms |
| D10-D36 | Benign neoplasms |
| D37-D48 | Neoplasms of uncertain or unknown behaviour |

Each type of malignant tumour listed above is a sub-category heading in its own right, under which specific underlying causes of death are listed. Here is part of the listing of underlying causes of death under the 'Skin' section of 'Neoplasms':

### C43-C44 Skin

| | |
|---|---|
| C43.0 | Malignant melanoma of lip |
| C43.1 | Malignant melanoma of eyelid, including canthus |
| C43.2 | Malignant melanoma of ear and external auricular canal |
| C43.3 | Malignant melanoma of other and unspecified parts of face |
| C43.4 | Malignant melanoma of scalp and neck |
| C43.5 | Malignant melanoma of trunk |
| C43.6 | Malignant melanoma of upper limb, including shoulder |

C43.7   Malignant melanoma of lower limb, including hip
C43.8   Overlapping malignant melanoma of skin
C43.9   Malignant melanoma of skin, unspecified

ICD-10 lists in total about 8,000 different underlying causes of death. National mortality statistics are produced by treating each of the 8,000 as a separate category and placing every death recorded in the state in the appropriate one. It will be noted in the examples given above that the ICD makes use of codes. Converting the underlying cause of death stated in a death certificate into a code consisting of one letter and three numbers — an alphanumeric code — is the key to producing national mortality statistics. The National Centre for Health Statistics in the United States provides computer software, called WinMMDS, which does all of the work of coding. The information in a death certificate is entered into a computer, word for word as it appears in Part I of the certificate. The computer application then selects the underlying cause of death and applies the appropriate code. This work, of course, can also be done manually, but most advanced countries now use the software developed in the USA.

Theoretically, any cause of death can be succinctly expressed in the four part code. If, for instance, you were hit by lightning on the golf course, your death would be coded for statistical purposes — no matter in what part of the world the golf course was situated, as: X33.3. The first part of the code stands for 'victim of lightning'; the last part '.3' translates as 'in sports and athletics area'. All forms of legal execution are coded as: Y35.5. Leprosy is A30.9.

ICD-10 is to be found on many internet sites. A searchable version is maintained by the WHO at:

http://www3.who.int/icd/vol1htm2003/fr-icd.htm?navi.htm+

which allows two kinds of search. First, you can input any cause of death term, such as 'leprosy', 'execution', etc. and the section covering that area will appear on screen, complete with the four character code. Secondly, you can input any code and the section which the code represents will appear on screen.

To test the versatility of the ICD-10, I attempted to code a selection of the deaths which occur in Shakespeare's play *Hamlet*. Hamlet's father, Old Hamlet, dies when his brother Claudius pours poison, 'juice of cursed hebona', into his ears while he is napping one afternoon in his garden; Polonius, while concealed behind an 'arras' or tapestry for purposes of eaves-dropping, is fatally stabbed 'through the arras' by Hamlet; Ophelia commits suicide by drowning herself in a river; Hamlet is killed after being wounded by a sword tipped with poison.

Had the events in Hamlet taken place in modern times, the American software in the Danish statistical office would have converted the information in the death certificates into ICD-10 codes as follows. Old Hamlet would have been covered by the code X89.04: 'assault by specified chemicals and noxious sub-stances'/ 'in the home, including garden to home'. Sometimes, an extra number may be added to the standard four characters to give some additional information. In this case the extra 4 stands for 'while sleeping'. The death code for Polonius would be X99.2, which means 'assault by sharp object'/ 'in a public administrative area'. Ophelia's code is X71.8, meaning 'inten-tional self-harm by drowning and submersion'/ 'in other unspecified area (river)'. Finally, Hamlet's own death code would be X85.0 'Assault by drugs, medicaments and biological substances'/ 'at home'. It is interesting to note that we will all end up with both a date of death and a four character 'underly-ing cause of death' code.

MORTALITY REPORTS

Annual national mortality compilations normally include sepa-rate statistics for men and women on all 8,000 underlying caus-es of death, for 21 age groups: beginning with under one year, ending with over 95 years and including 19 subdivisions in between, starting with age 1-4 years and rising in five year increments.

Published reports tend to combine codes into more general groupings, cutting down on detail and making the information more meaningful. The National Centre for Health Statistics in the United States, for instance, publishes annual mortality statistics for the USA under '113 selected causes of death'. The headings consist of a selection of ICD-10 chapter titles and sub-headings. All underlying causes of death fall into one or another of these categories. The UK annual mortality reports are based on a list of over 100 underlying cause of death categories.

Even the most cursory look at the USA mortality figures for the year 2002 gives a major insight into both the most likely causes of and the most likely ages at death for Americans. The top ten causes of death, and the percentages succumbing to each one, are:

| | |
|---|---|
| Heart disease | 28.5% |
| Cancer | 22.8% |
| Stroke | 6.6% |
| Chronic lower respiratory diseases | 5.1% |
| Accidents | 4.3% |
| Diabetes | 3.0% |
| Influenza/pneumonia | 2.6% |
| Alzheimer's disease | 2.4% |
| Nephritis | 1.6% |
| Septicaemia | 1.3% |

The ten leading causes combined account for 78.6 percent of deaths in the USA in 2002. More than half of all deaths are accounted for by the top two killers, heart disease and cancer. Of those who died in 2002, 74 percent were 65 years or older. If you concluded from this data that the average American can expect to die of either heart disease or cancer sometime after the age of 65, you'd be right more often than wrong.

Mortality statistics become much more meaningful when combined with census information. Then it becomes possible to make more accurate and refined predictions, with regard to the likely cause of and age at death for the various categories of people in a population

The modern census, that is, a periodic population count repeated every five or ten years, had its origins in the United States of America in 1790. Britain followed the example of its former colony in 1801. Today, the periodic census is an indispensable tool of governments everywhere. The modern census collects information about every citizen. Details such as age, sex, marital status, level of education and occupation are always collected. In some jurisdictions, other data may be requested where it is deemed to be relevant, such as race, religion and ethnic origin.

If the total number of people who died in a country in a particular year is known from the mortality data, and the total population of the country in the same year is also known from census data, it is possible to establish the annual death rate, usually expressed as so many people per 100,000 of the population. For example, in 2002, when the population of the USA was 289 million, a total of 2,443,387 people died, giving an annual death rate of 845.3 people for every 100,000 of the population. Separate death rates can also be calculated for different sections of the population. For instance, the death rates for men, women, various age groups, different races, etc, can all be computed. Using census and mortality figures, mathematicians called actuaries routinely calculate 'life expectancy' which indicates how long a person in a given population category can expect to live.

## LIFE EXPECTANCY NOW AND IN THE PAST

Census and mortality data have been available for many countries prior to the middle of the nineteenth century, allowing for the calculation of reliable life expectancy figures back as far as the 1840s. Efforts have also been made to guess at the life expectancy of people living further back in history, but the accuracy of those calculations is not reliable. The citizens of ancient Greece and Rome are said to have had a life expectancy of 28 years. It is believed that the Medieval English lived an average of 33 years. In 1900, world life expectancy was 30 years.

Improvements in life expectancy in the developed world have been dramatic in the course of the twentieth century, as evidenced by a comparison between the mortality figures for Britain at the start and those at the end of the century. Well over half the deaths at the beginning of the century occurred under the age of 45; infant mortality accounted for 25 percent of all deaths in 1901. By 2001, infant mortality accounted for less than one percent of deaths, and 96 percent of deaths occurred at the age of 45 and over. Deaths at the age of 75 and over accounted for only 12 percent of deaths at the beginning of the twentieth century, but by 2001, deaths in that age range constituted 65 percent of all deaths. There is a continuing small but steady increase in life expectancy from one year to the next, due to improvements in the treatment of the main killers: heart disease, cancer and stroke. While a male Briton born in 1901 would have had a life expectancy of 50, in 2006 that figure stands at a little over 76 years. The following life expectancy table, for Ireland, tells a similar story.

### Life Expectancy at Birth in Ireland from 1870 to 2002

| Year | 1870 | 1900 | 1930 | 1960 | 1990 | 2002 |
|---|---|---|---|---|---|---|
| **Male:** | 49 | 49 | 57 | 68 | 72 | 75 |
| **Female:** | 51 | 50 | 58 | 72 | 78 | 80 |

Life expectancy figures, like those in the table and paragraphs above, can be misleading. Basically, they are established by adding up the ages of all the people who died during a particular period, and dividing the sum total by the number of people.

It is simply an average. The figures quoted refer to life expectancy at birth. Much of the huge variation between the life expectancy figures at the beginning and the end of the twentieth century is due to the very high rates of infant and childhood mortality that prevailed in most places at the beginning of that period. Large numbers of deaths in childhood tended to depress the life expectancy figures. Many people who lived in areas with low life expectancy may have enjoyed long lives. Once they managed to get past the dangerous periods of infancy and childhood the main obstacles to attaining at least three score and ten were behind them.

WHEN WILL YOU DIE?

There is sufficient mortality and census data available nowadays to produce far more comprehensive life expectancy figures. In fact, most countries publish life expectancy tables covering every year of age from birth to 100 years and sometimes older. Separate male/female tables are produced due to the significant difference between the male and female lifespans. Women, on average, live about five years longer than men. The United States produces separate tables for whites and blacks for the same reason: the lifespan of whites is about five years longer than that of the black population. Apart from those significant differences, the tables produced by most of the affluent western democracies predict remarkably similar lifespans for their citizens at each year of life.

All such tables make it clear that your life expectancy increases as you grow older. For example, at birth, a male born in 2006 in the UK has a life expectancy of 76.26 years; if he reaches 30 he can expect a total lifespan of 77.43; and if he survives to his 65th birthday the table predicts that he will live beyond the age of 81. So, contrary to expectations, the longer you live, the longer you can expect to live! Some tables contain additional information apart from life expectancy, such as the probability of surviving from one year to the next, and the number of people remaining alive at the end of each year out of a notional starting population of 100,000.

YOUR LIFESPAN TABLE

The male and female life expectancy tables reproduced in the following three pages are based on United Kingdom data for the years 2002-2004. Figures from that jurisdiction are used because the United Kingdom is an advanced modern state with a very varied population, encompassing as it does, the peoples of England, Scotland, Northern Ireland and Wales, and many immigrants from all over the world. The figures, therefore, are representative of a significant segment of humanity. The figures are also very similar to those of other advanced western democracies. The first column lists age from one year to one hundred; column two gives the probability of not surviving for at least one more year; column three gives the number of survivors out of 10,000 born at year zero; and the final column gives the average lifespan for each year of age.

To find the information relevant to you, locate your age on column one and read the figures across the other columns. The inclusion, at each year of age, of a figure for the number of survivors out of an initial 10,000 helps to get a better understanding of how lucky or otherwise you are at each year of your life. For example, if you survive to the age of 79, though you will have surpassed by three years your life expectancy at birth, more than half the people who were born during the same year as yourself, will also be still alive.

## *What's Going to Kill You?*

Imagine yourself as part of a group of 10,000 people, either all male or all female. The members of your cohort were born in the same year, as yourself and enjoy the many health benefits of

# Your Death: when and how

| MALE | | | | FEMALE | | | |
|---|---|---|---|---|---|---|---|
| Age From | Chances of Dying This Year | Lives Left at Start of Year | Likely Life Span | Age From | Chances of Dying This Year | Lives Left at Start of Year | Likely Life Span |
| 0 | 0.57% | 10,000 | 76.3 | 0 | 0.47% | 10,000 | 80.7 |
| 1 | 0.04% | 9,943 | 76.7 | 1 | 0.04% | 9,953 | 81.1 |
| 2 | 0.02% | 9,939 | 76.7 | 2 | 0.02% | 9,950 | 81.1 |
| 3 | 0.02% | 9,936 | 76.8 | 3 | 0.01% | 9,948 | 81.2 |
| 4 | 0.02% | 9,934 | 76.8 | 4 | 0.01% | 9,946 | 81.2 |
| 5 | 0.01% | 9,933 | 76.8 | 5 | 0.01% | 9,945 | 81.2 |
| 6 | 0.01% | 9,932 | 76.8 | 6 | 0.01% | 9,944 | 81.2 |
| 7 | 0.01% | 9,930 | 76.8 | 7 | 0.01% | 9,943 | 81.2 |
| 8 | 0.01% | 9,929 | 76.8 | 8 | 0.01% | 9,942 | 81.2 |
| 9 | 0.01% | 9,928 | 76.8 | 9 | 0.01% | 9,941 | 81.2 |
| 10 | 0.01% | 9,927 | 76.8 | 10 | 0.01% | 9,940 | 81.2 |
| 11 | 0.01% | 9,926 | 76.8 | 11 | 0.01% | 9,939 | 81.2 |
| 12 | 0.01% | 9,925 | 76.8 | 12 | 0.01% | 9,938 | 81.2 |
| 13 | 0.02% | 9,923 | 76.8 | 13 | 0.01% | 9,937 | 81.2 |
| 14 | 0.02% | 9,922 | 76.9 | 14 | 0.01% | 9,936 | 81.2 |
| 15 | 0.03% | 9,920 | 76.9 | 15 | 0.01% | 9,935 | 81.2 |
| 16 | 0.03% | 9,917 | 76.9 | 16 | 0.02% | 9,933 | 81.3 |
| 17 | 0.05% | 9,914 | 76.9 | 17 | 0.03% | 9,931 | 81.3 |
| 18 | 0.07% | 9,909 | 76.9 | 18 | 0.03% | 9,928 | 81.3 |
| 19 | 0.06% | 9,902 | 77.0 | 19 | 0.03% | 9,926 | 81.3 |
| 20 | 0.08% | 9,896 | 77.0 | 20 | 0.03% | 9,922 | 81.3 |
| 21 | 0.07% | 9,888 | 77.1 | 21 | 0.03% | 9,920 | 81.3 |
| 22 | 0.08% | 9,881 | 77.1 | 22 | 0.03% | 9,917 | 81.4 |
| 23 | 0.08% | 9,873 | 77.1 | 23 | 0.03% | 9,915 | 81.4 |
| 24 | 0.08% | 9,865 | 77.2 | 24 | 0.03% | 9,912 | 81.4 |
| 25 | 0.09% | 9,857 | 77.2 | 25 | 0.03% | 9,909 | 81.4 |
| 26 | 0.08% | 9,849 | 77.3 | 26 | 0.03% | 9,905 | 81.4 |
| 27 | 0.08% | 9,841 | 77.3 | 27 | 0.04% | 9,902 | 81.4 |
| 28 | 0.09% | 9,832 | 77.3 | 28 | 0.04% | 9,898 | 81.5 |
| 29 | 0.09% | 9,824 | 77.4 | 29 | 0.04% | 9,895 | 81.5 |
| 30 | 0.10% | 9,815 | 77.4 | 30 | 0.04% | 9,891 | 81.5 |
| 31 | 0.10% | 9,805 | 77.5 | 31 | 0.05% | 9,887 | 81.5 |
| 32 | 0.11% | 9,796 | 77.5 | 32 | 0.05% | 9,882 | 81.6 |

# The Facts of Death

| MALE | | | | FEMALE | | | |
|---|---|---|---|---|---|---|---|
| AGE FROM | CHANCES OF DYING THIS YEAR | LIVES LEFT AT START OF YEAR | LIKELY LIFE SPAN | AGE FROM | CHANCES OF DYING THIS YEAR | LIVES LEFT AT START OF YEAR | LIKELY LIFE SPAN |
| 33 | 0.11% | 9,785 | 77.6 | 33 | 0.05% | 9,877 | 81.6 |
| 34 | 0.11% | 9,775 | 77.6 | 34 | 0.06% | 9,872 | 81.6 |
| 35 | 0.12% | 9,764 | 77.7 | 35 | 0.06% | 9,866 | 81.6 |
| 36 | 0.13% | 9,752 | 77.7 | 36 | 0.07% | 9,860 | 81.7 |
| 37 | 0.14% | 9,740 | 77.8 | 37 | 0.07% | 9,853 | 81.7 |
| 38 | 0.13% | 9,727 | 77.8 | 38 | 0.09% | 9,846 | 81.7 |
| 39 | 0.15% | 9,714 | 77.9 | 39 | 0.09% | 9,838 | 81.8 |
| 40 | 0.17% | 9,699 | 77.9 | 40 | 0.10% | 9,829 | 81.8 |
| 41 | 0.17% | 9,683 | 78.0 | 41 | 0.10% | 9,819 | 81.8 |
| 42 | 0.19% | 9,666 | 78.1 | 42 | 0.12% | 9,809 | 81.9 |
| 43 | 0.22% | 9,648 | 78.1 | 43 | 0.13% | 9,798 | 81.9 |
| 44 | 0.22% | 9,626 | 78.2 | 44 | 0.15% | 9,785 | 82.0 |
| 45 | 0.24% | 9,605 | 78.3 | 45 | 0.16% | 9,770 | 82.0 |
| 46 | 0.27% | 9,582 | 78.4 | 46 | 0.19% | 9,754 | 82.1 |
| 47 | 0.30% | 9,556 | 78.4 | 47 | 0.20% | 9,736 | 82.2 |
| 48 | 0.33% | 9,527 | 78.5 | 48 | 0.22% | 9,717 | 82.2 |
| 49 | 0.37% | 9,495 | 78.6 | 49 | 0.23% | 9,695 | 82.3 |
| 50 | 0.40% | 9,460 | 78.8 | 50 | 0.26% | 9,673 | 82.4 |
| 51 | 0.43% | 9,422 | 78.9 | 51 | 0.28% | 9,647 | 82.5 |
| 52 | 0.48% | 9,381 | 79.0 | 52 | 0.30% | 9,620 | 82.5 |
| 53 | 0.51% | 9,336 | 79.1 | 53 | 0.34% | 9,591 | 82.6 |
| 54 | 0.55% | 9,289 | 79.2 | 54 | 0.35% | 9,559 | 82.7 |
| 55 | 0.61% | 9,237 | 79.4 | 55 | 0.39% | 9,525 | 82.8 |
| 56 | 0.66% | 9,181 | 79.5 | 56 | 0.43% | 9,488 | 82.9 |
| 57 | 0.75% | 9,120 | 79.7 | 57 | 0.47% | 9,446 | 83.1 |
| 58 | 0.82% | 9,052 | 79.8 | 58 | 0.51% | 9,402 | 83.2 |
| 59 | 0.90% | 8,978 | 80.0 | 59 | 0.57% | 9,354 | 83.3 |
| 60 | 1.04% | 8,897 | 80.2 | 60 | 0.65% | 9,300 | 83.4 |
| 61 | 1.11% | 8,804 | 80.4 | 61 | 0.70% | 9,240 | 83.6 |
| 62 | 1.14% | 8,703 | 80.6 | 62 | 0.77% | 9,176 | 83.7 |
| 63 | 1.37% | 8,591 | 80.9 | 63 | 0.83% | 9,106 | 83.9 |
| 64 | 1.53% | 8,473 | 81.1 | 64 | 0.93% | 9,030 | 84.1 |
| 65 | 1.66% | 8,344 | 81.4 | 65 | 1.01% | 8,946 | 84.3 |
| 66 | 1.82% | 8,206 | 81.6 | 66 | 1.12% | 8,856 | 84.5 |

# Your Death: when and how

| | MALE | | | | FEMALE | | |
|---|---|---|---|---|---|---|---|
| AGE FROM | CHANCES OF DYING THIS YEAR | LIVES LEFT AT START OF YEAR | LIKELY LIFE SPAN | AGE FROM | CHANCES OF DYING THIS YEAR | LIVES LEFT AT START OF YEAR | LIKELY LIFE SPAN |
| 67 | 2.01% | 8,057 | 81.9 | 67 | 1.24% | 8,757 | 84.7 |
| 68 | 2.22% | 7,894 | 82.2 | 68 | 1.38% | 8,648 | 84.9 |
| 69 | 2.41% | 7,719 | 82.5 | 69 | 1.52% | 8,529 | 85.1 |
| 70 | 2.69% | 7,527 | 82.9 | 70 | 1.65% | 8,399 | 85.3 |
| 71 | 3.04% | 7,325 | 83.2 | 71 | 1.88% | 8,261 | 85.6 |
| 72 | 3.37% | 7,102 | 83.6 | 72 | 2.13% | 8,105 | 85.9 |
| 73 | 3.73% | 6,863 | 84.0 | 73 | 2.38% | 7,933 | 86.2 |
| 74 | 4.19% | 6,607 | 84.4 | 74 | 2.68% | 7,743 | 86.5 |
| 75 | 4.65% | 6,330 | 84.8 | 75 | 3.04% | 7,536 | 86.8 |
| 76 | 5.15% | 6,036 | 85.2 | 76 | 3.37% | 7,307 | 87.1 |
| 77 | 5.70% | 5,725 | 85.7 | 77 | 3.73% | 7,060 | 87.5 |
| 78 | 6.27% | 5,399 | 86.2 | 78 | 4.18% | 6,797 | 87.9 |
| 79 | 7.00% | 5,061 | 86.7 | 79 | 4.62% | 6,513 | 88.3 |
| 80 | 7.67% | 4,707 | 87.3 | 80 | 5.19% | 6,212 | 88.7 |
| 81 | 8.47% | 4,346 | 87.8 | 81 | 5.77% | 5,889 | 89.2 |
| 82 | 9.19% | 3,978 | 88.4 | 82 | 6.50% | 5,549 | 89.7 |
| 83 | 9.86% | 3,612 | 89.0 | 83 | 7.07% | 5,189 | 90.2 |
| 84 | 10.78% | 3,256 | 89.6 | 84 | 7.90% | 4,822 | 90.7 |
| 85 | 11.93% | 2,905 | 90.2 | 85 | 8.96% | 4,441 | 91.2 |
| 86 | 13.69% | 2,558 | 90.9 | 86 | 10.27% | 4,043 | 91.8 |
| 87 | 14.92% | 2,208 | 91.6 | 87 | 11.42% | 3,628 | 92.4 |
| 88 | 16.28% | 1,879 | 92.3 | 88 | 12.66% | 3,213 | 93.0 |
| 89 | 17.69% | 1,573 | 93.0 | 89 | 13.95% | 2,807 | 93.6 |
| 90 | 18.58% | 1,295 | 93.8 | 90 | 15.47% | 2,415 | 94.3 |
| 91 | 20.16% | 1,054 | 94.5 | 91 | 16.91% | 2,042 | 95.0 |
| 92 | 22.08% | 842 | 95.3 | 92 | 18.80% | 1,696 | 95.7 |
| 93 | 23.99% | 656 | 96.1 | 93 | 20.66% | 1,378 | 96.5 |
| 94 | 25.18% | 498 | 96.9 | 94 | 22.50% | 1,093 | 97.2 |
| 95 | 28.09% | 373 | 97.7 | 95 | 24.19% | 847 | 98.0 |
| 96 | 29.51% | 268 | 98.5 | 96 | 26.15% | 642 | 98.8 |
| 97 | 31.43% | 189 | 99.4 | 97 | 28.14% | 474 | 99.0 |
| 98 | 33.32% | 130 | 100.3 | 98 | 29.81% | 341 | 100.5 |
| 99 | 34.73% | 86 | 101.2 | 99 | 31.80% | 239 | 101.3 |
| 100 | 36.46% | 56 | 102.0 | 100 | 33.97% | 163 | 102.2 |

living in an advanced society. They are all keen to reach a ripe old age, to live, perhaps, to their hundredth year. You will see from the chart that the likelihood is that a total of 56 men and 163 women will survive to their hundredth birthday. The remainder will die *en route* from various causes. Statistics tell us how many are going to die at each stage of life and from what causes. A brief examination of the fate of the 10,000 as they pass through six age ranges should give a better understanding of the dangers that have been passed through and those that lie ahead.

INFANT (UNDER 1)
Deaths: Male: 57; Female 47
For 57 of the 10,000 males, their first year will also be their last year of life; 47 females will die. The first year of life is a dangerous period. Death is ten times more likely during this early developmental stage than at any of the other years of childhood. The same probability of death does not arise again until the mid-50s. Infant deaths are mostly caused by conditions associated with the first few months of life, conditions that are not easily classified and congenital malformations.

CHILDREN (1-14)
Deaths: Male: 21; Female: 17
Cancer is the main killer during childhood. Twenty percent of the deaths in the 1-14 age group are caused by malignant tumours. The brain, bone and cartilage, and the lymphoid system are the most common tumour sites. Another twenty percent of deaths are caused by accidents, about half of which involve land transport or drowning. Congenital malformations ranks as the third most significant cause, accounting for another ten percent of deaths. Cerebral palsy, epilepsy, pneumonia and meningitis are also ranked among the top ten killers. Homicide accounts for about two percent of deaths, ranking in about

eighth place. Since the number of deaths in this age range is small, the relative importance of some of the less significant factors may change from year to year.

TEENAGER/YOUNG ADULT (15-34)
Deaths: Male: 147; Female: 64
The most striking feature of deaths in this age group is that the number of male deaths is more than double that of females. Cancer continues to be the main female killer, with more than 23 percent of deaths attributable to it, and though the disease kills roughly the same number of males, it accounts for less than 10 percent of male deaths and ranks as the third leading cause. Suicide and road accidents are the two leading causes of male deaths, each accounting for about 20 percent of the total mortality. Killer number four and five for males, at 6 percent and 4 percent, are drug abuse and homicide. Clearly, many of the deaths in this group are related to lifestyle and cultural factors. Cirrhosis of the liver, often associated with excessive alcohol consumption, ranks as the sixth most common cause of death for both males and females.

ADULT (35-54)
Deaths: Male: 486; Female: 313
Though male deaths are numerically still well ahead of female deaths in this age range, the gap has narrowed considerably. Cancer is back as the number one killer for both sexes. A quarter of all male deaths are attributed to it and almost 47 percent of female deaths. Cancer of the breast is the cause of over 15 percent of deaths among women, while cancer of the lung and associated organs is the most prevalent form of the disease in men, causing about 5 percent of deaths. Heart disease is the number two killer of men: it accounts for 19 percent of mortalities; followed by cirrhosis of the liver which accounts for 10 percent of deaths. Heart and liver disease are also among the

top three killers of women, each accounting for about 7 percent of female deaths. Suicides account for a smaller percentage of deaths than in the earlier age group, amounting to 8 percent of male deaths and less than four percent of female deaths. However, a significantly greater number of both men and women commit suicide in the 35 to 54 age range. The percentages are lower because the overall number of deaths has risen. On the other hand, though accidents, as a leading cause of death, is in the top ten list of killers, the number of males killed in road accidents has dropped significantly. A new entry into the top five killers of both men and women, cerebrovascular diseases, accounts for about 5 percent of all deaths.

MIDDLE AGE (55-74)
Deaths: Male: 2,682; Female: 1,816
The five main causes of death in this age group are the same for men and women. They are: cancer, heart disease, cerebrovascular diseases, chronic lower respiratory diseases, and influenza and pneumonia. Combined, they cause 75 percent of deaths in this age group. Women suffer significantly more from cancer than men (43 percent in women and 38 percent in men) and men suffer more from heart disease than women (24 percent in men and 14 percent in women). Diabetes has entered the top ten killers for both men and women, and 'dementia and Alzheimer's disease' ranks as number 8 for women, killing 1.2 percent.

OLD AGE (75 AND OVER)
Deaths: At this stage, 6,607 of the 10,000 males and 7,743 of the 10,000 females are still alive – they will all die during this open-ended period.

This is the only category in which more women than men die. This is due to the fact that they have survived in greater numbers to reach the final age group category. It has no upper age limit. Everyone in the group will eventually die. It is interesting to note that over 66 percent of males and more than 77 percent of females are expected to live beyond the age of 75. The top ten killers are listed below separately for men and women. The percentages of deaths for which each is accountable are also given.

MALE

| | |
|---|---|
| 1. Malignant Neoplasms (cancer) | 23.6 |
|    of trachea (windpipe), bronchus and lung | (5.3) |
|    of prostrate | (4.5) |
|    of colon, sigmoid (lower colon), rectum and anus | (2.5) |
| 2. Ischaemic heart diseases (inadequate blood supply to the heart) | 21.5 |
| 3. Cerebrovascular diseases (problems with the arteries supplying blood to brain) | 11.1 |
| 4. Influenza and Pneumonia | 7.4 |
| 5. Chronic lower respiratory diseases | 6.7 |
| 6. Dementia and Alzheimer's disease | 3.2 |
| 7. Heart failure and complications and ill-defined heart diseases | 2.7 |
| 8. Aortic aneurysm and dissection (weakening, bulging and tearing of the aorta, the biggest artery in the body) | 2.4 |
| 9. Diseases of the urinary system | 2.0 |
| 10. Parkinson's disease (also known as shaking palsy) | 1.4 |
|    All other causes | 18.0 |

FEMALE

| | |
|---|---|
| 1. Ischaemic heart diseases (inadequate blood supply to the heart | 17.1 |
| 2. Malignant Neoplasms (cancer) | 16.3 |
|    of trachea (windpipe), bronchus and lung | (2.7) |
|    of breast | (2.4) |
|    of colon, sigmoid (lower colon), rectum and anus | (1.9) |

3. Cerebrovascular diseases
  (problems with the arteries supplying blood to brain) 14.6
4. Influenza and Pneumonia                                9.2
5. Dementia and Alzheimer's disease                       6.0
6. Chronic lower respiratory diseases                     4.3
7. Heart failure and complications and
  ill-defined heart diseases                              3.6
8. Diseases of the urinary system                         2.1
9. Accidents                                              1.6
10. Aortic aneurysm and dissection
  (weakening, bulging and tearing of the aorta,
  the biggest artery in the body)                         1.3
All other causes                                         23.9

## Recalculate Your Life Expectancy

How close will you get to a three digit lifespan? Will you rank among those who fell early on or will you be among the last of your generation? Your predicted lifespan as it appears on the chart is simply the average lifespan of a person of your age. Many people do not conform to the average. They may beat the odds and enjoy a longer life, or may be cut down sooner than expected. Luck is a factor in determining whether you get more time or less than what the chart seems to promise. Luck cannot be quantified, but several other significant factors that influence length of life can. Several 'life expectancy calculators' are available on the internet. They pose a series of questions related to genetic inheritance, social status, physical environment and lifestyle. The answers attract positive or negative marks in the form of numbers of years to be added or subtracted from the basic life expectancy figures that appear on the chart. The following questions, and the marks, are based on three life-expectancy quizzes: Age Venture:

www.demko.com/deathcalculator.htm

Life Expectancy Calculator:
>www.msrs.state.mn.us/info/Age_Cal.htmls
and The Life Expectancy Calculator:
>www.fis.org/public/obiterdicta/lecalclhtml

## REFINE YOUR LIFESPAN ESTIMATE
Genetic Inheritance:
- +1 for each grandparent who lived to the age 80;
- −1 for each parent or grandparent who died before age 50 of heart attack, cancer or stroke;
- −1 if a brother or sister suffered from cancer or a heart condition while under the age of 50.

Social Situation:
- +1 if you are a college graduate or have a professional qualification;
- +3 If you live with a spouse or friend;
- −1 for every 10 years of living on your own;
- −1 if your income is below the national average.

Environment
- +1 if you live in an advanced technological society;
- −1 if you live in an emerging industrial society;
- −1 if you live in a polluted area.

Life Style:
- −1 if you are up to 14 pounds underweight; or
- −2 if you are more than 14 pounds overweight;
- −1 for every 10 pounds of excess body weight;
- −1 if you regularly skip meals or regularly consume junk food;
- +1 if you eat high fibre food daily;
- +1 if you drink one or two alcoholic drinks per day;
- −1 for every two additional alcoholic drinks per day;

−2 if you sleep less than 5 hours or more than 9 hours per night;

−6 if you smoke more than 40 cigarettes per day; or

−4 if you smoke 20-40 cigarettes per day; or

−2 if you smoke 10-20 cigarettes per day; or

−1 if you are a passive smoker, that is, regularly inhale the cigarette smoke of others;

−1 if your job and life are sedentary;

+1 if you engage in vigorous exercise at least three times per week;

+1 if you are easygoing;

−1 if you are aggressive, intense and easily angered;

+1 if you are happy;

−1 if you are unhappy.

+1 if you are mentally active;

−1 if you are depressed and bored.

Medical Factors

−2 if you are on long-term therapeutic drugs with known side-effects;

+2 if you go for an annual medical check-up.

RECALCULATION

When you tally your score, you could find yourself in the happy position of being able to add up to 20 extra years to your life expectancy; however, if your lifestyle is unhealthy and your ancestors were short-lived, you might have to subtract up to 20 years.

Though all of the items on the list have an indisputable bearing on health and longevity, the exact amount of time each one may add to or subtract from a person's life is uncertain. It might be wise to take a less mathematical view, and to regard the factors mentioned above as positive or negative indicators.

## Healthy Life Expectancy

The steady rise in life expectancy over the last hundred years has to be regarded as a very positive development. However, the huge increase in the elderly portion of the population in developed countries has created problems, mainly related to the fact that there is a major difference between life expectancy, on the one hand, and healthy life expectancy, on the other. Research has shown that at the age of 65 men can expect a further twelve healthy years of life, but also four years of poor health; women at age 65 can look forward to thirteen healthy years and six years of ill health. Several studies have indicated that as life expectancy increases, a progressively bigger portion of the extra time gained will be spent in a state of ill health. From the point of view of society and even more from a personal perspective, this is a frightening prospect with huge financial implications.

The measure of healthy life expectancy used in some countries is the number of years a person could expect to live independently without major limitation in lifestyle and without requiring the assistance of another person. Healthy life expectancy is often referred to as 'independent life expectancy'.

Life expectancy quizzes, as well as giving a more accurate prediction of total lifespan, often act as a wake-up call. Confronted by the fact that unhealthy habits, such as smoking, excessive drinking, over-eating, mental and physical laziness, reluctance to seek medical advice and habitual negative emotions reduce lift expectancy, prudent people start to make changes, adopting more sensible, life enhancing habits. The concept of healthy life expectancy is a further incentive to turn over a new leaf. Unhealthy habits, particularly obesity, accentuate the impact of most illnesses, converting a bigger proportion of life expectancy to years of disability and dependency.

# 3. Does it Hurt?

D read of death is a combination of many different fears. One of the most worrying is the prospect of having to endure acute and prolonged physical pain: a drawn out death. This chapter examines various kinds of distress associated with the terminal period of life and the methods used to alleviate them. In particular, it looks at the kind of death that gives ample notice of its arrival, that is preceded by progressive disablement, and is usually accompanied by moderate to severe pain: in other words, the classic death by cancer.

The focus is on cancer for a number of reasons. In the previous chapter, reference was made to the 8,000 different categories under which deaths are recorded. Given the wide range of symptoms associated with such a variety of ways of dying, it is not possible to be comprehensive nor to generalise too much on the topic of pain and death. Cancer is one of the top two causes of death worldwide. For example, it accounts for a little over 25 percent of all deaths in Ireland and Britain, and a little under that figure in the USA. One in every eight deaths in the world, a total of seven million per year, is due to cancer. The end of life experience of people vanquished by other major diseases is not dissimilar to the experience of cancer patients. Also, much of the information available on pain and dying is based on the treatment of cancer patients. The principles of pain management in cancer patients are applicable to patients dying from other causes as well.

## *Varieties of Pain and Discomfort*

An estimated 90 percent of cancer patients experience significant physical pain during their illness. They may also suffer emotionally, mentally and spiritually.

Physical pain is often divided into three categories. Visceral pain originates in the internal organs, especially the abdomen; sharp, cramping, achy and throbbing, it can be difficult to pinpoint its exact place of origin. Somatic pain is more clearly localised in muscle, skin and bone, and can also be sharp, achy and throbbing. It is the most common kind of pain experienced by cancer patients. Pain associated with the nervous system — neuropathic pain — radiates out from a central point and is sharp, tingling, burning, shooting or stabbing.

The intensity and duration of pain varies. Pain can be mild, moderate or severe. Pain that lasts for a long time, whether mild or severe, is described as 'chronic'. The term 'acute' is frequently used in relation to pain; it means severe pain that lasts a relatively short time. Breakthrough pain is a term used to describe acute pain suffered by a patient already on pain medication. It is common for patients who have had limbs or other body parts amputated to feel 'phantom pain' apparently originating in the missing parts.

Other kinds of physical distress associated with dying include: various kinds of disability, nausea, headache, dizziness, drowsiness, weakness, fatigue, stiffness from inactivity, shortness of breath, loss of appetite, digestive problems, constipation, diarrhoea, incontinence and skin breakdown. The psychological well-being of dying patients may be undermined by feelings of helplessness and hopelessness, anxiety, stress, anger, irritability, depression, crying, mood swings, social isolation, confusion and suicidal feelings.

Spiritual crisis is another cause of anguish at the end of life. The decline in religious practice and belief has meant that people must figure out their place in the universe for themselves. A busy life provides little time for philosophical reflection. People may only start to think about the meaning of life after they get confirmation that they are close to the end of it.

## CAUSES OF PAIN

Pain is normally an indication that bodily tissue is being damaged in some way. Chronic pain in cancer patients is primarily due to the effects of the cancer itself. The type and stage of the disease often determines the exact kind of pain experienced. A growing tumour can cause pressure on nearby organs, nerves and bone, but can also cause pain in parts of the body remote from it by obstructing blood vessels and restricting blood circulation. A tumour can block tubes within the body, producing a variety of pain-generating problems. In the later stages of cancer, secondary tumours may develop far from the original site, multiplying the disease's pain creating capacity.

Sometimes pain is caused by the methods used to treat the cancer, such as surgery, radiation and chemotherapy. Occasionally, pain may be unrelated to either the disease or the treatment. Like everybody else, cancer patients suffer from everyday pain, such as headache and toothache.

## SELF ASSESSMENT

Pain is subjective. Nobody can feel your pain except yourself. A doctor may check it out by giving a thorough physical examination, but the principal way of assessing a patient's pain is by asking the patient to describe it. An enlightened doctor will accept the description and prescribe accordingly. It is no longer acceptable for a doctor to override the patient's assessment, to diagnose a 'low pain threshold' and to withhold medication.

Because pain is what you say it is, you need to be able to describe it accurately to be assured of getting the appropriate treatment. Conveying the intensity of your pain is of primary importance. It is normal to describe intensity on a scale of one to ten. Zero — which is off the scale — represents a painless state and the number ten represents the most excruciating pain imaginable. Numbers 1-3 stand for mild pain, numbers 4-6 represent moderate pain, while the numbers 7-10 indicate severe pain.

You must also be able to describe other characteristics of your pain, such as what it feels like. Words like dull, sharp, throbbing, steady, and stabbing are useful in this context. Other important factors that should be clarified are: where you feel it, when it began, how long it lasts, whether it is constant or variable, how often it comes per day, whether it affects your ability to function or prevents you from doing certain activities, what relieves it and what makes it worse.

The control of pain is very important during terminal illness. When medication starts, remembering all the details of how your pain was affected by it may be difficult. For this reason, keeping a pain diary is often recommended. Details to be recorded include the level of the pain before and after medication, the time of taking the medication and dose, how long it works for, side effects, activities that you were more capable or less capable of doing, and any other factors that could be regarded as significant. Family and friends can help with these details by giving feedback on how you appeared to them.

## *Ways of Relieving Pain*

With proper treatment, successful pain relief can be achieved in about 90 percent of dying patients, allowing them to remain comfortable, alert and to interact with family and friends in their last weeks of life. However, some studies have shown that, for one reason or another, less than half receive adequate treatment for their pain.

The best way to treat pain is to find the cause and deal with it. This often involves shrinking a tumour in order to remove a blockage or to relieve pressure on adjacent bodily parts. Surgery, radiation and chemotherapy are the principal means of reducing the size of tumours. Radiation is particularly useful for zapping tumours which develop in the bone and bone marrow, and the procedure often substantially relieves severe pain. When none of these methods can be used or when the cause of the pain is not known, various pain relief methods are tried.

METHODS OF TREATMENT

The principal method of treating pain is the use of pain killers, also known as analgesics. Drugs called opioids, which are derived from opium, are used extensively in treating acute and chronic pain. Non-opioid drugs are used for treating less severe pain and are sometimes used in partnership with opioids.

Non-drug methods of pain relief have also been found useful, either on their own or in conjunction with drug therapy. Some are rather simple techniques such as distraction therapy which involves absorption in some activity which takes attention away from the pain. This approach to pain relief can be as simple as reading a good novel. The use of imagery is a variation of the distraction method. Visualising a beautiful or peaceful landscape can divert the mind from a suffering body. Hypnosis, which is an advanced, assisted form of distraction, has been found to give some respite as well. Techniques like these, which involve concentrated mental activity, do not work very well when energy levels are low.

Some pain relief techniques are purely physical. Massage helps to reduce pain. So too does transcutaneous electrical nerve stimulation (TENS), a treatment which uses an electric current to soothe the nerves. Acupuncture has been used for thousands of years in Chinese medicine. It was found to be so proficient in the relief of pain that it has been used to anaesthetise patients during surgery. A remarkable film clip, which has been broadcast on TV many times, of a Chinese patient eating an orange while a surgeon removes his appendix, testifies to the formidable power of this ancient oriental procedure. In extreme cases, nerves may be cut by a surgeon, stopping pain messages being relayed to the brain.

People of a meditative and philosophical cast of mind may be interested in an approach to terminal pain suggested by Stephen Levine in his book *Who Dies*. His work has been described by Elizabeth Kubler-Ross – the woman who brought death out of the closet – in the following manner: 'Stephen's work is magic. His work with the grieving and dying is amongst the most skilful and compassionate that I am aware of'. Levine's outlook is heavily influenced by Zen Buddhism, a philosophy which includes belief in reincarnation. Such a mysterious doctrine may put the more conservative reader off reading the book, however, his insights into the workings of the human mind are thought provoking. He urges people to be always present in their lives, to move beyond reward orientated behaviour and to develop an awareness of the great space in the mind beyond mere consciousness of the self. He states that the anticipation of pain and the fear and avoidance of pain serve only to amplify pain, and suggests that the best course is to engage with the pain. He includes five 'pain meditations' which direct the reader's attention to the pain they are experiencing. Focusing on pain enables the reader, more than likely for the first time, to explore the nature of pain, to face it, and possibly feel it in quite a different way. Levine is not necessarily urging the reader to forsake pain-killers, but it is clear from the experiences of many of the terminal patients mentioned in his book, that the different perspective he was able to give them was very helpful. Less fear and lower doses of pain-killers were the usual outcome.

DRUG TREATMENT

The World Health Organisation (WHO) has developed a three-step 'ladder' for cancer pain relief. The plan recommends that: 'if pain occurs, there should be prompt oral administration of drugs in the following order: non-opioids (aspirin and paracetamol); then, as necessary, mild opioids (codeine); then strong opioids such as morphine, until the patient is free of pain. To calm fears and anxiety, additional drugs – "adjuvants" – should be used.' Adjuvants, in this context, are drugs whose primary function is not the relief of pain, but which help to do so in some situations. They include tranquillisers and anti-depressants. This pain-relief model may also be applied to the treatment of pain caused by other conditions as well as cancer.

The WHO plan also recommends that to maintain freedom from pain, drugs should be given 'by the clock', that is every 3-6 hours, rather than 'on demand' or 'as required'. Additional drugs should be available for the treatment of breakthrough pain, should it occur. This three-step approach of administering the right drug in the right dose at the right time is inexpensive and 80-90 percent effective.

It is not the stage of terminal illness but the level of pain that determines which medicine to use. To ensure that a patient reaches the right step of the ladder promptly, the effect of the drug that is administered is closely monitored and adjustments are made every 24-48 hours. If non-opioids at the lowest rung of the ladder do not stop the pain, the dosage can be increased, but not by very much because this kind of medication, beyond a certain level, can cause kidney damage. Weak opioids are tried next. Since they are often mixed with non-opioids, they too have a maximum limit which is soon reached and cannot be safely exceeded. However, on the third rung of the ladder —

opioids — can be safely increased by up to 50 percent every 24 hours until satisfactory relief is achieved. Doctors properly trained and experienced in the treatment of pain are not reluctant to use strong opioids such as morphine in high doses to achieve satisfactory results.

## *Opioids and How They Work*

Opium has been used for the relief of pain for thousands of years. Though pain can still be sensed while under its influence, it ceases to be felt as a distressing and unpleasant sensation. The drug can be uplifting and may produce feelings of overall invigoration and euphoria and a sense of increased power and confidence. Opium and its derivatives are unique among pain-killers in that neither sensory perception nor physical co-ordination are impaired unless the drug is taken in high doses. It seems to sharpen rather than befuddle the intellect. The effects of alcohol are often unfavourably compared to those of opium.

Because consciousness is located in the brain, everything you experience is essentially in your head. A pain in any part of the body must be transmitted along a network of nerves until it reaches the brain, otherwise, the pain does not register. Certain parts of the brain specialise in receiving pain signals. The body produces chemicals called endorphins which can attach themselves to the pain receptors and prevent the pain messages from getting through. They are released into the bloodstream in response to pain. As well as being natural pain-killers, endorphins also produce feelings of euphoria. Athletes performing at the edge of human endurance sometimes experience the sensation of breaking through the pain barrier. The agony of extreme exertion triggers a shot of endorphins. Relief is accompanied by feelings of elation. Laughter and sex are also known to increase the endorphin levels in the blood stream.

The problem with endorphins is that neither the quantity nor the timing of their release are under conscious control. The value of opioids is that they contain chemicals which are almost identical to the body's natural pain blockers. In fact, the word 'endorphin' was coined from the term 'endogenous morphine', that is, morphine created within the body. Whether ingested, injected or inhaled, the active molecules in opioids get into the circulation system, pass through the blood-brain barrier and attach themselves to pain receptors, allowing euphoria and analgesia to be produced on demand and to the desired degree.

Unfortunately, opioids attach themselves to other brain receptors as well, impacting negatively on some important bodily functions and producing undesirable side effects. Opioids can suppress the coughing reflex and cause breathing to become slow and shallow. A sufficiently high dose can stop breathing altogether, resulting in death. Vomiting and nausea is a common side effect, especially after the initial dose of an opiate, but tolerance soon builds up. For centuries, opium was valued as a cure for diarrhoea as it retards the rate of involuntary muscular contraction of the intestines. Frequent use of opioids causes constipation. Opium and all its derivatives reduce the sex drive. But perhaps the biggest fear associated with this powerful range of drugs is the danger of addiction.

In the hands of trained medical personnel, none of the side effects of opioids present serious difficulties. Appropriate medication can be given to prevent nausea and vomiting. Constipation is always anticipated and is easily treated by a change of diet and the use of laxatives. Breathing problems rarely arise; in fact opioids are the drugs of choice for the treatment and relief of shortness of breath. Research has shown that addiction to prescribed opioids as a consequence of using them for the relief of severe pain is very rare. Drug-seeking behaviour in patients who have been inadequately medicated may be mistaken for addiction. Such behaviour is not addiction, however, it is an understandable craving for pain relief. The craving ceases when the right dose is given. In true addiction, the focus on drugs does not cease, rather it escalates.

## *Opium: for Pleasure and for Pain*

Despite its unrivalled pain suppression qualities, the use of opioids arouses suspicion, feelings often shared by patient, family and doctor. Mistrust and unease may lead to hesitation, and reliance on less effective pain relief measures, or on lower than effective doses. We live in times when the term 'narcotic', which is defined as a substance taken for the relief of pain, seems to be associated with crime and the police rather than medicine and doctors. Opium and its derivatives, such as morphine, bring words like 'junkie' and 'addict' readily to mind, with accompanying imagery of complete human debasement. Under these circumstances it is not surprising that the idea of taking opioids, frightens people.

Throughout the course of history, opium and related drugs seem to have been used as much for pleasure as for pain. The ancient Greeks were familiar with it. In the *Odyssey*, Homer describes an incident in which opium is mixed with wine to cheer up Telemachus, son of Odysseus. It had the power of: 'robbing grief and anger of their sting and banishing all painful memories. No one who swallowed this dissolved in their wine could shed a single tear that day, even for the death of his mother or father, or if they put his brother or his own son to the sword and he were there to see it done'. Almost three Millennia later, Thomas de Quincey was extolling the virtues of opium in the same terms in his *Confessions of an English Opium Eater*. The therapeutic and recreational use of opium seemed to have co-existed quite happily with one another for thousands of years.

In the course of the twentieth century, strict governmental

control of drugs has criminalised all recreational use. Rather than stamping out such use, this course of action has resulted in the handing over of the drugs trade in most countries to criminal gangs. More importantly, it has confused people who are in need of strong medication. For this reason, it is worthwhile pausing here to have a brief look at the history of opium. A little background information on opioids often helps to allay people's fears.

## HISTORY OF OPIUM

It is hard to believe that in the twenty-first century substances derived from the opium poppy, *Papaver somniferum*, are still the principal means of relieving severe pain. There is some evidence that Neanderthal man may have used the poppy as a remedy for pain as far back as 30,000 years ago. The earliest written references to the red medicinal flower appear around 4000 BC. The annals of the ancient world, including those of Egypt, Greece and Rome, chronicle the importance of 'the plant of joy' to mankind. Harvesting opium is not much different today to the way it was done in the ancient Egyptian capital of Thebes three thousand years ago. After the poppy petals have fallen off, incisions are made in the plant's large seed pods. Overnight, milky sap oozes out forming a dark resin which can be scraped off and collected. The raw opium can then be used, processed or stored for long periods.

Opium was taken in many different forms. Ancient peoples either ate parts of the flower or converted them into liquids to drink. A difficulty associated with the latter was that the active ingredients in opium do not dissolve readily in water. Classical Greek physicians either ground the whole plant or used opium extract. The Turks discovered that the most potent components of the drug could be absorbed by burning it and inhaling the smoke. Smoking was the method favoured by the Chinese for many centuries. The sixteenth century physician known as

Paracelsus developed a way of making opium more readily available in liquid form which involved combining it with brandy. He found that alcohol easily absorbed the essential parts of the drug. He called the new concoction 'laudanum'. By the nineteenth century, proprietary brands of laudanum were widely available to all who wanted it and without prescription. Harassed mothers used it to sedate babies and fractious children. Brand names like Godfrey's Cordial, Street's Infants' Quietness, Atkinson's Infants' Preservative, and Mrs Winslow's Soothing Syrup all contained opium and were formulated especially for children. Orphanages also used opium products as a cost saving measure: the drug is known to act as an appetite suppressant.

In 1803, a German scientist named Friedrich Sertürner isolated the active ingredient of opium. A simple chemical process allowed him to extract and purify this substance and to dispense with ninety percent of the bulk of the raw opium. He gave the name 'morphine' to the new, concentrated product, calling it after Morpheus, god of sleep. Forty years later the invention of the hypodermic needle and syringe allowed for the rapid delivery of morphine. Injecting the drug brought instant relief and an impact three times more powerful than that produced by ingesting it.

The nineteenth century was the heyday of opium. Vast quantities were exported to China by British merchants. When the emperor of China banned its use and importation in 1839, the British Empire fought a war to keep the market open. The Chinese were defeated and were forced to sign a treaty in 1842 allowing the opium trade to continue. A second opium war started in 1856 due to western insistence on expanding the opium market. Again, the Chinese suffered defeat and opium poured into China in such quantities that by the end of the nineteenth century, an estimated quarter of the adult male population were addicted. There was widespread addiction in other countries as well. Liberal use of morphine during the American

Civil War in the treatment of wounded soldiers from both sides of the divide resulted in a nationwide addiction problem.

In 1895, the German pharmaceutical firm, Bayer, developed a purified version of morphine. They began to market it three years later, introducing it at the same time as the company's most famous brand of medication: aspirin. Both products often appeared in the same advertisements. The morphine based drug was called 'heroin'. It was promoted as 'the sedative for coughs' and was available in many forms, including heroin pastilles, heroin cough lozenges and heroin tablets. As a cough suppressant, it was widely used in the treatment of tuberculosis. The powerful feelings of euphoria which it also produced must have been some consolation for those suffering from what was a terminal disease at that time. Also among its suggested uses was the treatment of morphine addiction. Gradually, stories about its own highly addictive nature began to appear in the medical press. By 1903, heroin addiction was rising at an alarming rate. Heroin is now generally banned and unavailable even on prescription.

## Double Effect and Terminal Sedation

Fortunately for terminally ill patients, other opium derivatives are legal and readily available for the relief of pain. However, in some situations, opioids may not work. What happens to terminally ill patients suffering severe pain, unrelieved by the strongest medication available? The answer depends very much on the doctor, and perhaps on instructions left by the patient or given by the patient's representative. The doctor can take the humanitarian view: that the maximum dose of morphine for a cancer patient in pain is the dose that will relieve the pain, and proceed to administer a dose large enough to kill the pain but which could also depress the patient's breathing and hasten death. Taking such a measure would not offend against accepted legal, moral or ethical code. The doctrine of 'double effect' is the justification. This concept is based on medieval Christian moral theology. In this context it means that the procedure is permissible because the intention and the effect of the treatment was the relief of suffering, and that the hastening of death, the second effect of the action, was wholly unintended. In rare cases, a last resort therapy called 'terminal sedation' may be used for patients whose suffering cannot be relieved in any other way. A patient is given sufficient medication to induce unconsciousness and kept in that condition until death occurs naturally as a result of the illness or disease. Under these circumstances, all artificial life supports are also withdrawn. This procedure is also justified by the double effect doctrine.

## Euthanasia and Assisted Suicide

Many people believe that the ultimate painless death is achieved by assisted suicide or euthanasia. The doctrine of double effect, however, cannot be expanded to justify either euthanasia or assisted suicide. It can be reasonably applied only in a very narrow range of circumstances: a terminally ill patient suffering unbearable pain, unrelieved by safe doses of medication. Those who argue in favour of euthanasia claim that death in the modern world is worse than death in times gone by.

In the past, people died quickly from infectious diseases; now, in the developed Western World, they die slowly from chronic diseases. Today's killers, heart disease, cancer, stroke and diabetes, may involve months or years of debilitating illness. In the past, people generally died at home; now three quarters of people die in institutions such as hospitals and old people's homes, incrementally losing freedom, independence and self-confidence; becoming more isolated and confused; clocking up huge medical bills. Modern medical science can sustain a twilight life long beyond the point at which most people would opt for death, at least when they think about it from the perspective of full health. The plight of the disabled elderly and the position of terminal patients who cannot get adequate pain relief inevitably turn people's attention to the drastic solutions of assisted suicide and euthanasia.

In most parts of the world, both of these actions are classified as homicide. Up to recent times, suicide and attempted suicide were treated as serious crimes in many jurisdictions. Attempted suicide was a crime in Ireland up as far as 1992. It is perfectly legal to refuse medical intervention. Intravenous feeding, supplementary oxygen, chemotherapy, antibiotics, blood transfusions and all other such procedures may be refused by right. A patient suffering from kidney failure may discontinue dialysis, an action which guarantees death within one week. The law denies the same patient access to a drug overdose which would bring about a swifter and less distressing demise.

Mercy killing tends to be debated passionately, and both sides of the controversy can advance strong arguments. The point is often made that people can be talked into euthanasia by grasping relations who see their inheritance being gobbled up by medical expenses. The weak and the sick may not be able to resist the demands of bullying relatives and may agree to condemn themselves to death. A state, top heavy with old people, might find euthanasia to be a prudent way of reducing the medical expenditure required by this dependent element of the population. On the other hand, the drastic actions taken by those who are desperate for death are very affecting. One man who was partly paralysed and dying from cancer used the only means at hand to kill himself: he set himself alight with fuel from a cigarette lighter. A patient connected to a ventilator managed to unplug the machine and died from suffocation, choked by the air tube in his throat.

In some cases, a ban on euthanasia leads directly to suicide. If you cannot give instructions to medical professionals to end your life when your illness reaches a particular stage, you might decide to end it yourself while you still have the capacity to do so. The author Arthur Koestler and Nobel prize-winning physicist Percy Bridgman both committed suicide precisely for this reason, as is evident from their suicide notes. Terminal patients often feel much more comfortable, secure and relaxed when they have within their grasp the means of killing themselves: pills in the locker, gun under the pillow.

Surveys in the USA have shown that public opinion is tending to favour the legalisation of assisted-suicide and euthanasia. Opinion polls in the United Kingdom consistently show that more than 80 per cent of the British public also support such a change in the law. Despite the danger of criminalising themselves, some medical professionals have admitted to assisting patients to die.

FIGURE 3:
HIPPOCRATES, THE FATHER OF MEDICINE: HIS OATH INCLUDES THE LINES 'I WILL KEEP THEM [THE SICK] FROM HARM AND INJUSTICE…I WILL NEITHER GIVE A DEADLY DRUG TO ANYBODY WHO ASKS FOR IT, NOR WILL I MAKE A SUGGESTION TO THIS EFFECT.'

## EUTHANASIA IN THE NETHERLANDS

Should a measure be passed into law, legalising euthanasia, it is likely that it would be modelled on the policy adopted in the Netherlands. There, euthanasia is understood to mean termination of life by a doctor at the request of a patient. Such doctors can not be prosecuted, provided they satisfy the statutory 'due care' criteria and notify death by non-natural causes to the appropriate regional euthanasia review committee. The main aim of the policy is to bring matters into the open, to apply uniform criteria in assessing every case in which a doctor terminates life, and hence to ensure that maximum care is exercised in such cases. Pain, degradation and the longing to die with dignity are the main reasons why patients request euthanasia. Cost of treatment is not a factor since the Dutch health care system is accessible to all and guarantees full insurance cover for terminal and palliative care.

When dealing with a patient's request for euthanasia, doctors in the Netherlands must observe the following due care criteria. They must: be satisfied that the patient's request is voluntary and well-considered; be satisfied that the patient's suffering is unbearable and that there is no prospect of improvement; inform the patient of his or her situation and further prognosis; discuss the situation with the patient and come to the joint conclusion that there is no other reasonable solution; consult at least one other physician with no connection to the case, who must then see the patient and state in writing that the attending physician has satisfied the due care criteria; exercise due medical care and attention in terminating the patient's life or assisting in his/her suicide.

The vast majority of cases of euthanasia, 90 percent, relate to terminal cancer patients. Since children also suffer from this disease, the Act allows twelve to fifteen-year-olds to request euthanasia, but requires parental consent for it to be performed. It permits sixteen and seventeen-year-olds to make such life and death decisions for themselves, although it prescribes that their parents must always be involved in the discussions. Eighteen year olds are regarded as adults.

A doctor may only perform euthanasia on a patient in his care. He must know the patient well enough to be able to assess whether the request for euthanasia is both voluntary and well-considered, and whether his suffering is unbearable and without prospect of improvement. Two thirds of the requests for euthanasia that are put to doctors are refused. Treatment frequently provides relief, while some patients enter the terminal stage of their illness before a decision has been reached. Doctors are not obliged to comply with requests for euthanasia. Experience shows that many patients find sufficient peace of mind in the knowledge that the doctor is prepared to perform euthanasia and that they ultimately die a natural death.

ASSISTED SUICIDE IN THE UNITED STATES

Physician-assisted suicide (PAS) has been legal in the state of Oregon since November 1997 under the Death with Dignity Act. Oregon is the only part of the USA in which such measures are lawful. The Act allows terminally ill Oregon residents to obtain prescriptions for lethal medications from their physicians for self-administration. Under Oregon law, the procedure is not regarded as suicide, nor is it considered to constitute mercy killing or homicide. The term 'physician-aided suicide' is used in the Act because that is the terminology used in medical literature to describe the practice. The Act specifically prohibits euthanasia, where a physician or other person directly administers a lethal dose.

To request a prescription for lethal medication, the Death with Dignity Act requires that a patient must be an adult resident of Oregon who is capable of making such a decision, and who has been diagnosed with terminal illness that will lead to death within six months. The request must be made to a licensed Oregon physician. The patient is required to make two oral requests, at least fifteen days apart, and a written request signed in the presence of two witnesses. The prescribing physician must confer with a consulting physician and also apprise the patient of alternatives before complying with the request. A physician must make a written report to the Department of Human Services of all prescriptions for lethal medications. Neither physicians, pharmacists nor health care workers are obliged to participate in the scheme.

From its inception in 1997 up to the end of 2005, 246 patients took lethal doses. As a group, their profile differed somewhat from the characteristics of the general population who died from the same underlying causes. The people who took their own lives tended to be younger, though in excess of 65 percent were still over the age of 65 years; more likely to be divorcees or people who never married; and to have higher than average educational attainments. Cancer and HIV/AIDS sufferers were more inclined to opt for PAS. Males and females were equally represented. In nearly all cases, reasons given for wishing to end life included: a decreasing ability to participate in activities that make life enjoyable, loss of dignity, and losing autonomy. Medical costs appears not to have been a factor as almost all patients had some form of medical insurance.

In the year 2005, 64 prescriptions for lethal doses of medication were issued; 32 patients did not take the medication, of those, 15 died from illness and 17 were still alive at year's end. Six who received the medication in 2004 took it in 2005, making a total of 38 PAS deaths for that year. All of the lethal prescriptions were for barbiturates (mostly pentobarbital and secobarbital). Three patients experienced complications after ingesting the fatal dose: two vomited some of the medication, one of whom died 15 minutes after ingestion, the other after 90 minutes. The third became unconscious 25 minutes after taking the medication, regained consciousness after three days and died two weeks later of the underlying illness. These difficulties may have resulted from the fact that physicians are not legally required to be present when a patient takes the medication. All but two of the 38 patients died at home. Though up to 17 percent of terminal patients considered the option, the number of physician-assisted suicides remains small, accounting for about 1 in 800 deaths in Oregon in 2005.

SWITZERLAND: THE ONLY SUICIDE DESTINATION
Oregon, the Netherlands, Belgium and Switzerland are the only parts of the world in which a person may be openly and legally assisted in committing suicide. In other parts of the globe, prosecution may follow such activities. In Britain, conviction for rendering such assistance could result in up to 14 years imprisonment. Assisted suicide is also a crime in the Republic of Ireland, and in 2003 legal proceedings were initiated against an American Unitarian minister for allegedly assisting in the suicide of a woman. Though the case did not result in a conviction, it served as a warning. In other jurisdictions, whereas there may not be a law specifically against assisted suicide or euthanasia, people engaging in such activities may still be charged with crimes such as manslaughter or homicide. The laws in Oregon, the Netherlands and Belgium relating to assisted suicide and euthanasia are framed in such a way as to prevent foreigners and non-residents from availing of their provisions. Switzerland alone does not bar foreigners.

The Zurich-based charity, Dignitas, assists foreigners who come to Switzerland to end their lives. The organisation has helped more than 450 people to commit suicide since its foundation in 1998, including at least three Irish people and 42 Britons. A death arranged by Dignitas costs €3,500. The cost includes counseling, all administrative fees and payments to those assisting. It does not include the cost of the one-way ticket to Switzerland. The organisation is genuinely non-profit making because the Swiss law states that: 'whoever lures some-one into suicide or provides assistance to commit suicide out of a self-interested motivation will, on completion of the suicide, be punished with up to five years' imprisonment'.

Dignitas assisted suicides take place in a fourth floor apart-ment in Zurich, which has a kitchen, a living room and a 'dying room'. A doctor and an assistant are present for the procedure, but the last act of either swallowing the drug or opening a valve of a drip, is carried out by the patient. Typically, the assistant mixes 12 grams of sodium pentobarbital in a glass of water, offers it to the patient, pointing out that: 'if you drink this, you will sleep two to five minutes and then you will die'. After swallowing the drink, the patient is helped to a bed, will fall asleep and go into a deep coma. Twenty to thirty minutes later, the patient will be dead.

Many Swiss are concerned about the impact of the activities of Dignitas on the reputation of their country and there is a pos-sibility that the law on assisted suicide may be changed to exclude foreigners in response to this dissatisfaction. Beatrice Wertli, of the Swiss Christian Democrats, has been quoted as saying: 'we do not want Switzerland to be a destination for tourism for suicide'.

# 4. Dying, Dying, Dead

The last words of King Charles II were: 'I have been a most unconscionable time dying but I beg you to excuse it'. Having suffered a stroke, the king took a full four days to die. He felt embarrassed that his courtiers should be detained round his deathbed for so long. By today's standards, though, four days is quite short notice. Modern diagnostic procedures can detect the symptoms of serious illness long before they become a major problem. Chronic conditions, such as congestive heart failure, can give five years' advance warning. The rate of progress of cancer can often be accurately tracked, allowing the date of death to be predicted reasonably accurately. Patients are routinely informed when their condition reaches the stage known as terminal illness: a term that is now generally understood to mean that death is likely to occur within six months. Consequently, dying now has two meanings: the original meaning as understood by King Charles, and a more lengthy period of time during which the patient may be able to function normally.

## *Five Stages*

Elizabeth Kubler-Ross was one of the first people to study the process of dying. In her book *Death and Dying*, now regarded as a classic, she identified five stages that people go through after being told that their illness is terminal: denial, anger, bargaining, depression and acceptance. The five stages taken together constitute a kind of grieving for the loss of oneself.

Mourning for another person seems to follow the same course. It may seem difficult to imagine how denial fits into this context. It is easy to visualise concealment of knowledge of terminal illness, even from oneself, but pretending that a loved one has not died would seem to constitute altogether bizarre behaviour. However, a few generations ago, the death of a close family member was often treated precisely in that manner. After the return from the cemetery, it was not unusual for the name of the deceased never to be mentioned in the house again. The family entered a kind of conspiracy of silence to protect themselves against the pain of bereavement.

In fact, most bad news is absorbed gradually, and roughly in the same five stages. Denial comes first. How many times have you heard 'I don't believe it', as the initial response to an unpleasant occurrence? Imagine going to pick up your car only to discover that it's not in the place you parked it. It's gone. You don't accept that it's been stolen. You look for it in other nearby places, knowing for sure that you will not find it; you return several times to check again whether it is back where you left it, you try to figure out other reasons to explain its disappearance. The denial stage passes quickly and then you become angry: 'what kind of world are we living in! Who would take…' The bargaining begins after that: 'if I get it back, the first thing I'll do is install a good alarm system…I'll never again park a car in this area…' Depression sets in: 'that's it, the car is gone. I'll have to walk home, contact the insurance company,

expect a hike in my premium…' Finally, the stage of acceptance is reached: you get a taxi to the police station.

If you were to be informed of your own imminent death, you
would probably absorb the news in much the same manner, but
more slowly. The stages may overlap, or may occur simultaneously, or stages already experienced may recur. It is also possible that you may respond in a different way altogether: reaction
to dying is not a rigid process. Well meaning people may try to
rush you through the putative stages, to speed up your arrival at
acceptance. This would not be helpful. You do not need to get
angry or to engage in bargaining or to accept that you are going
to die. Many people never get past denial and, as a stratagem
for dealing with terminal illness, denial has its advantages.

DENIAL

The American poet Emily Dickinson may have had denial in
mind when she said: 'The Truth must dazzle gradually / Or
every man be blind'. Denial is the equivalent of a pair of sun-
glasses, offering protection against a painfully blinding truth. It
is a coping mechanism, albeit a temporary one. Denial acts as
a defence against unpleasant realities, keeping them out of conscious awareness. It gives a terminal patient the space to come
to terms with the situation using a self-selected timeframe.

Doctors may collude in a patient's denial by giving the terminal prognosis in terms that are not so stark, allowing the patient
to digest the information slowly, and to return after a few days
to ask questions that will elicit the whole of the bad news. Of
course, some doctors may withhold information simply to avoid
an emotional scene. A patient's family members may reinforce
denial if they find it difficult to cope with the situation. There
is a lot to be said for denial and patients should not be forced out
of that position simply as a matter of course. However, denial
may become a negative and dangerous course of action if taken
too far, and may lead to the patient undertaking futile medical

treatments and failing to put important affairs in order, such as the making of a will. Denial usually disappears with the progress of the disease.

## ANGER

When a person begins to realise that death is certain, anger, resentment, envy and rage replace denial. These strong feelings can be directed against the doctor who gives the bad news, the nursing staff, members of the family or anyone who has dealings with the patient. Anger is contagious. Carers can often have a tough time holding their temper in check when they have to put up with a hostile response to all their attempts at being helpful and supportive. But it must be remembered that a terminal patient is responding naturally to loss. If your life savings were stolen, a negative emotional response would be anticipated. A person suffering from terminal illness has suffered a vicious larceny: the robbery of all their future years.

## BARGAINING

During this stage, efforts are aimed at reversing the diagnosis. Religious people try to barter with God by making undertakings to do various good deeds or to make amends for past misdeeds in return for a reprieve. Even people who are not regular church goers may find themselves trying to bargain with a higher power in more or less the same terms. The medical staff may be involved by the patient, for instance, volunteering for new, experimental treatments: I'll risk my life to further medical science so that I may be rewarded with an extension of life.

## DEPRESSION

Symptoms worsen, energy levels drop and dependence increases. Denial no longer works, anger is futile, bargaining gained nothing. The patient begins to feel beaten. The response is depression. This reaction is due both to the mounting problems associated with the illness and the impending death. Compared to earlier stages, this period is rather quiet.

ACCEPTANCE

The final stage is not necessarily a happy time of reconciliation to one's fate and with one's family. This period may be characterised by a decreased interest in communication, even with close family members, by a desire to be left alone, and by a lack of interest in worldly events. Often, the family may have hoped for a different script at this time: a tying up of all loose ends followed by a *bon voyage* deathbed scene in the Hollywood tradition; but the wishes of the dying person should be given precedence.

Tranquillisers may have a role to play in dealing with the strong emotions associated with the 'five stages'. A person who is a worrier, is likely to become very anxious when confronted with the reality of death. Depression and anxiety are best treated with medication and assurance.

# Signs of Imminent Death

Certain kinds of behaviour are often observed in people shortly before death which give notice that the end is not too far off. An obvious sign is the focusing on finalising affairs, such as making a will, and straightening out insurance and other financial issues. People also show an interest in taking care of personal matters such as catching up with friends, and patching things up with family members. In the last weeks or months, people are inclined to seek solitude, withdrawing from social activities and remaining at home much of the time. Often, there is a loss of interest in daily activities, including eating and drinking, and increased periods of inactivity, lethargy and sleep. Anxiety may increase causing restlessness, and sometimes confusion. People often refer to the fact that they are going to die, or ask questions about death. A dying person may request to speak with a clergyman. Some people talk about seeing family and friends who are already dead.

Sometimes, there is a marked change in personality, accompanied by wild behaviour, severe agitation or hallucinations. On the other hand, a dying person may not move for long periods of time, may complain of feeling numb, and the hands, feet, arms and legs may feel very cold to touch and have a blotchy purple or blue appearance. It may become increasingly difficulty to rouse a dying person and a coma-like state may be entered. Physical signs of approaching death include bruises, infections, and wounds that fail to heal; swelling of parts of the body, especially at the extremities such as the ankles; apnoea, that is the suspension of breathing for several seconds, which may happen both during sleep and while awake.

Every death is individual. Some people die quickly giving very little advance indication. To ensure that someone does not die alone, a family member or friend should be at the bedside at all times. A practical reason for such a presence is to attend to the patient's comfort. Whereas symptoms like shortness of breath may be relieved by medical staff by suctioning of fluid from the lungs, provision of supplementary oxygen, and administering opioids; a simple measure such as adjusting the patient's position in the bed – which can be done by family or friend – may also offer relief.

Dying enters a more active phase in the last few days of life. In some cases this period extends to a couple of weeks. Food and drink may be refused either, due to difficulty in swallowing – even liquids – or due to loss of appetite. This is not necessarily a bad thing. Fasting may be beneficial and may play a role in dying comfortably. Restricted fluid intake reduces swelling round tumours. As the heart and kidneys fail, a normal liquid intake causes fluid to lodge in the lungs. This contributes to shortness of breath, which can be very distressing. Major changes in respiration develop, characterised by longer periods of apnoea and abnormal breathing patterns such as cycles of slow then fast breathing. There is a decrease in urination and the urine darkens in colour. Blood pressure drops. An inability to speak and loss of hearing, feeling, smell, taste or sight may develop at the final stage.

A rather delicate question that often arises too, is whether a dying person urinates or defecates on the point of or immediately after death. The answer, in nine out of ten cases, is no. When it does occur, it may simply be an indication that the body was able to relax enough to do so before finally shutting down. Moving a body after death can result in the expulsion of fecal matter, but this is normally caused by pressure on the abdominal area compressing the bowels

If you are suffering from a terminal illness, it would be prudent to anticipate the symptoms of dying and to leave clear instructions as to how they should be treated. Family members may take a view that may not be in the best interests of the patient. They may be distressed at the idea of discontinuing nutrition and hydration, and may opt to have the patient fed intravenously or via a tube through the nose, especially if the patient is expected to live for a few more days. They may also demand a limit to the use of opioids in the treatment of shortness of breath for fear that the high doses necessary to fully treat the symptoms would hasten death. It is best to make your views on these topics known to your doctor and your family well in advance.

People often feel confused about how to behave at a deathbed. They feel foolish talking to someone who is clearly unconscious. However, it may be important. It has been noticed on many occasions that death does not take place until the dying person has been given 'permission' to depart. In Ireland, it was customary to say the rosary round the death bed, and time after time people noticed that death seemed to occur with the completion of the final decade. People have been known to 'hang on' until a relative who had to travel from afar arrives on the scene. Many experts believe that a dying person is aware of what is going on, despite appearances to the contrary. For this reason, whatever about talking to the dying, people are advised that crying and grieving should be avoided. The purpose of a presence at the death bed is to provide comfort and a peaceful atmosphere.

At the very end, death may not be so bad. Woody Allen is quoted as saying, 'It's not that I'm afraid to die... I just don't want to be there when it happens', and in a sense, many people manage to achieve this paradoxical state, because in their final days, about half of all terminally ill patients lapse into unconsciousness for most of the time.

## Death

The cessation of breathing and heartbeat, the unmistakable signs of death, are soon followed by other changes. The whole body turns pale, as the redundant blood drains through capillaries from the upper surfaces and gathers in the lower blood vessels. Temperature drops. *Rigor mortis*, the characteristic stiffening of the dead, sets in about three hours after death and lasts for about thirty-six hours. Twelve hours after death, the body is cool to the touch. Core temperature continues to drop until after about twenty-four hours it reaches the temperature of its surroundings. Contrary to popular belief, neither hair nor nails continue to grow after death. The appearance of growth is due to post mortem shrinkage of the skin which gives more prominence to nails and facial stubble.

After a patient has been pronounced dead, the body is wrapped in a sheet or shroud and transported to the morgue, where it may be held in a refrigeration unit until it is released to the family or an undertaker acting on their behalf, or in some instances, sent for autopsy.

## THE DEAD

In the course of a lifetime, most people in the developed world will never get the opportunity of touching a corpse, apart from the token kiss on the forehead or cheek of a loved one before the closing of the coffin. The work of preparing the body is carried out by undertakers. Specialists in the trade prepare it for viewing. Their job is to make the deceased look as lifelike as possible, in other words, to disguise the fact that the person is dead. Under these circumstances it is not easy for people, especially children, to develop an understanding of death. Rosy-cheeked grandad is being buried in his best suit with a faint smile on his face! Even adults find it hard to reconcile this situation with the concept of death.

Up to the recent past, things were very different. Most people died at home. As the body cooled, whitened and stiffened, you perceived the void that divides the living from the dead. Preparing the corpse for burial was a matter for the family. As the body was being washed, you felt, with a shock, the coldness of the flesh, the dead weight of the head and limbs. The lifelessness of the deceased was even more evident when the corpse was manhandled into the coffin. The venue for viewing the body by neighbours and friends was the home, where it remained, at least overnight. You had time to contemplate the stillness of the corpse; to conclude by personal observation that the loved one was gone and that the corpse was just a sad, inanimate reminder. You were ready to let go by the time the funeral came round. By then, burial could only be regarded as a logical imperative.

Members of the medical profession still have an old fashioned familiarity with the dead, acquired in dissection rooms during their first years at medical school. They are unlikely to regard a corpse with awe and reverence. The gap between the contrasting attitudes of the general public, on the one hand and the the medical profession on the other, towards dead bodies, has been the cause of some painful misuderstandings in the past, particularly in relation to autopsies.

In 1998 the Bristol Enquiry was set up in response to a public outcry against the manner in which the bodies of children were treated after death in the Bristol Royal Infirmary. Without parental knowledge or consent, hearts had been systematically taken from the bodies of children undergoing post mortem examinations at the hospital. The organs had been used for research, medical education, or simply put into storage. A follow up inquiry established that these procedures were common practice in many other British hospitals as well.

The Madden inquiry investigated a similar medical scandal in Ireland and issued its report in 2005. Among its recommendations was the establishment of an education and information programme: 'to ensure that members of the public are informed as much as possible as to the post mortem procedures, the value of the retention of organs and tissue, the importance of pathology practices in our healthcare system, the value of post mortems in the education of medical professionals...'

The various medical tribunals have helped to give doctors a better understanding of the sensitivities of the bereaved. However, they have done little to alter the public's naïve concept of death and its aftermath. A general ignorance about death extends beyond the hospital gates to the undertaker's funeral parlour and to the process of decomposition in the graveyard. Both of these areas will be visited in later chapters, but it seems appropriate to include a description of an autopsy in this chapter, as that procedure takes place, if it is deemed necessary, immediately after death.

AUTOPSY

The purpose of an autopsy is to ascertain the cause of death. The procedure may be ordered by the authorities for that purpose. It is always required in the case of a suspicious death. An autopsy may also be requested by the family of the deceased, but hospitals may not carry out the procedure of their own accord. A full post mortem examination requires the removal – followed by the further dissection – of all of the internal organs, including the brain. Clearly, it is a highly invasive process.

Autopsies are not uncommon. It is estimated that the procedure is currently performed in the case of one in every ten deaths in the USA. Nevertheless, this is a major drop since the 1950s when half of all deaths resulted in autopsy. The figures have dropped dramatically for two reasons. First of all, it is becoming increasingly difficult to get family consent. Secondly, studies have consistently shown that in the case of 20 to 40 percent of patients on whom autopsies were performed, treatable conditions were detected that had gone undiagnosed. Such discoveries could easily lead to litigation and this is likely to have caused doctors to lose their enthusiasm for the procedure.

In England and Wales, about 130,000 autopsies are conducted annually, which means that about a quarter of all bodies are subjected to the procedure. In Northern Ireland about 1,500 autopsies are carried out each year.

The bodies of some of the most famous and most beautiful people were subjected to this destructive but necessary procedure, including that of Marilyn Monroe and President John F. Kennedy.

An autopsy is normally carried out in a purpose built suite. The main item of furniture in the dissecting room is the autopsy table, a waist-high, slanted tray large enough to accommodate a human body lying on its back. The table edges are raised to keep blood and other fluids from spilling onto the floor. It is plumbed for running water to facilitate washing away whatever fluids are released during the procedure.

The body is spread, face up, on the table, and a 'body block' of rubber or plastic is placed under the back. This protrudes the chest, and allows the arms and neck to fall back making it easier for the pathologist to work. Abnormalities of the external body surfaces are noted and described, either by talking into a voice recorder or making notes on a diagram and/or checklist. Then the work begins in earnest. At this point, any squeamish person present would probably leave the room; squeamish readers might now take the cue to skip ahead to the next chapter.

The pathologist makes a Y-shaped incision stretching from the chest to the pubic bone. The arms of the 'Y' extend from the front of each shoulder to the bottom end of the breastbone. In women, these incisions are diverted beneath the breasts, making the overall shape more like a 'U' with a tail. The 'tail' cut goes from the sternum to the pubic bone, typically making a detour round the navel. The incision is very deep, cutting down to the bone in the chest region, and cutting right through the thick, fleshy wall in the abdominal area.

The skin, muscle and soft tissues of the chest wall are peeled back with the aid of a scalpel. When complete, this 'V' shaped

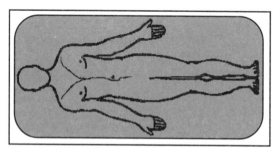

FIGURE 4: THE PATHOLOGIST MAKES A Y-SHAPED INCISION…

chest flap is pulled upward over the face of the corpse. The abdomen is further opened by dissecting the abdominal muscle away from the bottom of the rib cage and diaphragm. The flaps of the abdominal wall fall off to either side, exposing the abdominal organs.

A bone cutter, similar to a curved pruning shears, is used to cut up each side of the rib cage. In this way, the chest plate, consisting of the sternum and the ribs which connect to it, is detached from the rest of the skeleton. The chest plate is lifted off, with the aid of a scalpel if additional cutting is necessary.

The pathologist then works from the neck downwards, cutting whatever connective tissues attach the main organs to the body. A cut is made above the larynx – the part of the respiratory tract containing the vocal chords – allowing the windpipe to be pulled downward into the chest cavity. The scalpel is used to free up the remainder of the chest organs from their attachment at the spine. The diaphragm – the muscle separating the chest cavity form the abdominal cavity – is cut away from the body wall, and the abdominal organs are pulled out and down. Finally all the organs of the trunk are removed from the body in one connected mass and placed on a dissection table for further examination.

The body block is removed from beneath the corpse's back and placed under the back of the head to give it more elevation. Then an incision is made, right to the bone, running from behind one ear, over the crown of the head and continuing as a mirror image down the other side. The skin and soft tissues are divided into a front flap and a rear flap. The front flap is pulled forward over the patient's face and the back flap is pulled backwards over the nape of the neck. In this way, the whole top hemisphere of the skull is exposed. The pathologist saws round the skull and then eases the skull cap off with a special chisel, fully exposing the brain. After cutting the spinal cord, the whole brain is easily lifted out.

The attention of the pathologist now turns to the bloc of organs on the dissecting table. Each of the main organs is separated and detached from the mass. The heart, lungs, kidneys, liver, etc are weighed and examined externally. They are then dissected for more detailed examination. The heart and kidneys are cut open and the lungs and liver are sliced into thin sections with a 12 to 18 inch 'bread knife'. The brain is usually dealt with in the same way, unless it requires detailed investigation, in which case in must be given special treatment to firm it up. This involves suspending it by a string in a jar of formalin for a period two to three weeks. The chemical preserves and solidifies this soft and easily deformed organ, making it easier to handle in the subsequent examination. The intestines are removed and opened over a sink under running water, so that all the faeces and undigested food flow out. This step is extremely offensive to the nose.

Postage stamp sized pieces of tissue are sliced from each organ. These samples are used to make slides for microscopic examination. Additional slices are kept in a 'save jar', typically a one-quart or one-pint jar filled with formalin, as backup. Labs keep the save jar for a variable length of time, but at least until the final written report is prepared. Some labs keep the save jar for years. All tissues that are disposed of are done so by incineration.

After all of the above procedures are performed, the body is now an empty shell, with no chest, abdominal or pelvic organs and no brain. The front of the rib cage is also missing. The scalp is pulled down over the face, and the whole top of the head is gone.

In the process of reassembly, the skull cap is placed back in position. The original cut is always notched to aid accurate replacement. The scalp is then pulled back over it, and the wound sewn up. The notch also ensures that the top of the skull will not slip off afterwards. The wound is now a line that goes from behind the ears over the back of the skull, so that when the head rests on a pillow in the coffin, the wound is not visible.

In many institutions, the sliced organs are poured back into the open body cavity. In other places, the organs are incinerated. In either case, the chest plate is placed back in the chest, and the body wall is sewn back up, so that the final wound again resembles a 'Y'.

A complete autopsy, as described above, may not always be necessary. Sometimes, a limited autopsy, in which the head is excluded, or a selective autopsy in which specific organs only are examined, may suffice. Autopsies normally include testing for infections, changes in body tissue and organs, and chemicals like medication, drugs and poisons.

Finally, the body is rinsed off with a hose and sponge, covered with a sheet, and made available for collection by the family or their agents.

# 5. Dead Beyond Doubt

'**D**eath', according to the first edition of *Encyclopaedia Britannica*, published in 1768, 'is generally considered as the separation of the soul and body; in which sense it stands opposed to life, which consists in the union thereof'. While this definition fitted in reassuringly with the philosophical outlook generally held at that time, it was of no practical assistance in the actual diagnosis of death. There was no obvious means of ratifying when exactly the separation of body and soul was complete and a person was dead. Death had to be established by observing that breathing and heartbeat had ceased and assuming that the cessation was permanent. From time to time this method was found to be unreliable, a factor which contributed to the widespread fear – common throughout the eighteenth and nineteenth centuries – of being buried alive.

In the twenty-first century, we are faced with, perhaps, a greater problem in relation to the diagnosis of death. The extensive use of life-support systems in intensive care units of hospitals means that we now have several different definitions of death. Currently, death is understood to mean: either irreversible cessation of circulatory and respiratory functions – the traditional view – or the irreversible cessation of all functions of the entire brain including the brain stem. In the United Kingdom, a patient may be certified as being dead when the brain stem alone is deemed to have stopped working permanently. Cessation of breathing and blood circulation is established by observation, as in the past, but both brain death and brain stem death are difficult to verify as no single test can be relied upon.

FIGURE 5: THE DANCE OF DEATH (ALSO KNOWN AS *LA DANSE MACABRE*, *LA DANZA MACABRA* AND *DER TOTENTANZ*): IN THE LATE MIDDLE AGES, DEATH WAS OFTEN PERSONIFIED AS A SKELETON INVITING PEOPLE OF ALL AGES AND ALL CLASSES TO DANCE. SUCH ART WORKS REFLECT BOTH THE FRENZIED DESIRE FOR ENTERTAINMENT AT A TIME WHEN LIFE WAS 'NASTY, BRUTISH AND SHORT', AND THE CONSTANT PRESENCE OF DEATH — MEDIEVAL PEOPLE HAD TO SUFFER THE DEPREDATIONS OF WARS, FAMINES AND THE BLACK DEATH, AS WELL AS THE NORMAL HAZARDS OF HUMAN MORTALITY.

This chapter casts an eye back on the fears of premature burial that worried our ancestors, and examines whether we should still be concerned about the same possibility today.  It also reviews current controversies about death, provoked by new definitions of death and by cutting edge medical technologies.

## *The Past*

According to Dr Jan Bondeson in his 2001 book, *Buried Alive: The Terrifying History of Our Most Primal Fear*, a widespread dread of premature burial gripped continental Europe in the eighteenth century, which intensified and spread to the UK and America in the nineteenth century.  The original stimulus to this fear was a Latin treatise, in which it was claimed that 'many apparently dead, have afterwards proved themselves alive by rising from their shrouds, their coffins, and even from their graves'.  The thesis attributed premature burials to unreliable means of determining death.  The dreadful possibility of live internment proved to be an irresistible theme, especially when it was given a less scholarly treatment by the French writer Jean-Jacques Bruhier.  His book was translated into several languages and spread beyond the bounds of his native France to other Western European countries.

In 1790, in response to the growing fear, a German physician named Christopher Wilhelm Hufeland, suggested the erection of 'a house for the dead', in his hometown of Weimar.  There, the bodies of the dead could rest until the only indisputable evidence of death – putrefaction – became evident.  The idea was taken up with enthusiasm and 'leichenhauser' as they were called, were constructed in many parts of Germany and in other countries as well.

The Frankfurt leichenhaus was fairly typical.  It consisted of a warder's room, where an attendant was always on duty.  On each side were five rooms, well ventilated, kept at an even temperature, and each provided with a stand on which a corpse could be laid. On one of the fingers of each corpse a ring was placed which was connected by a string to a bell which hung outside the warder's room. The warder was expected to be constantly on the alert for the ringing of the bell. The bodies were inspected at regular intervals by a medical officer. One revival, that of a child, was said to have taken place at Frankfurt.

Many leichenhauser continued to operate well into the twentieth century. As well as ensuring that there was not the remotest possibility of live burial, they also offered a respectable place for the reception of the dead and removed the corpse from the dwellings of their grieving families. As soon as putrefaction begun, the relatives assembled in one of the halls adjoining the leichenhaus, and the obsequies took place.

Leichenhauser were not the only response to the fear of premature burial. Various mechanisms were produced which purported to allow a person who was buried alive either to escape or to draw attention to his predicament. George Bateson, an Englishman, designed a simple device which proved popular. The end of a string, which was connected via a pipe to a bell above ground, was put in the hand of the deceased. A very slight movement of the hand would ring the bell and summon help. Bateson's invention was advertised in rather exaggerated terms: 'a most economical, ingenious, and trustworthy mechanism, superior to any other method, and promoting peace of mind amongst the bereaved in all stations of life. A device of proven efficacy, in countless instances in this country and abroad'. Despite the hype, there is not one recorded instance of Bateson's device resulting in saving a life.

Apparently, fear of premature burial weighed particularly heavily on the Teutonic mind. Prior to 1901, sixteen US patents for devices offering escape from such a predicament were issued to men with Germanic surnames. Each of the inventions included a bell or flag mounted on the surface connected to the coffin through a pipe. The devices were reusable since they could be removed once death was certain.

There are many reported cases of premature burial, or near escapes from such a fate. Thomas A Kempis the thirteenth century author of *The Imitation of Christ*, was never made a saint because, it was said, when they dug up his body – in order to bring his bones to the ossuary – it was discovered that there were scratch marks inside the lid of his coffin. It was concluded that he had not been reconciled to his fate! Many of the 'buried alive' stories refer to the remote past and their authenticity cannot be verified. Some are the equivalent of urban legends.

For example, there is a widespread belief that Ann Carter Lee, mother of General Robert E. Lee, commander-in-chief of the Confederate Army, was buried alive in 1805. According to a story published in *The Washington Post* of 1934, four physicians pronounced her dead when they failed to detect a heartbeat. The funeral was held and the remains were put in the family vault. A week later when the sexton entered the Lee mausoleum at Stratford, Virginia, to put fresh flowers on the casket, he heard her cry for help. She soon revived, regained her health and 15 months later, gave birth to her famous son. However, the authenticity of the story has been questioned. Ann Lee's eldest son, Charles Carter Lee, wrote many recollections of his early life at Stratford, yet he never mentioned anything about his mother's alleged premature burial. Other family members and researchers have also rebutted the story, including Douglas Southall Freeman who produced the definitive General Lee biography. Freeman wrote letters of refutation to newspapers that published the story. The tale seems to have been concocted by a Kentucky man who claimed to be Robert E. Lee's cousin.

It may become necessary to relocate cemeteries from time to

time. The consequent mass exhumation of bodies reveals for inspection hundreds of corpses in various states of decay. Occasionally, what appears to be evidence of premature burial is reported. These signs include blood staining and scratching on the inside of the coffin lid, and bodies in radically different positions from those in which they were buried. However, the dynamics of decomposition can account quite adequately for these worrying signs. During the process of decomposition, trapped gases swell up the entire body and the bodily tissues begin to liquefy. Pent up gases force fluids out through the nose and mouth. Pressure may build up to such a level that organs literally explode, resulting in staining and a change of position: signs that could be mistaken for violent efforts at escape from the grave.

Ignorance of the same processes probably gave rise to another popular myth – the existence of vampires. Bodies exhumed in the first weeks after death appear to bear the marks of the 'undead', signs which include: blood flowing from the mouth and nose and the body developing a plump and well-fed appearance. It is easy to conclude that after dark, the undead come fully to life, rise out of their graves to drink the blood of unwary sleepers, returning at dawn, plumper and with some of their liquid nourishment dribbling down their chins – as seen in many horror films.

## *THE PRESENT*

The fear of premature burial is largely a thing of the past, though it is still possible to be pronounced dead prematurely. People tend to be more scientifically aware these days and realise that the amount of air in a coffin could not sustain life for very long. Lingering for days in the close confines of a coffin and frantically trying to break out and claw your way to the surface is just not possible. The meagre supply of oxygen would run out quickly, resulting in a swift death. Also, in many countries embalming is now a routine procedure. The embalming process, which drains the blood and replaces it with the poisonous chemical formaldehyde, makes live burial impossible.

DEATH DIAGNOSIS
Death is normally diagnosed by means of five simple tests which establish the absence of vital signs:

1. The absence of a carotid pulse: if the rhythmic contraction and expansion of the two large arteries that supply blood to the head and neck cannot be detected for a period of thirty seconds, it is an indication that the circulation of the blood has ceased.

2. The absence of respiratory activity for 30 seconds: this is established by observation.

3. The absence of heart sounds for 30 seconds: a stethoscope is normally used for this purpose.

4. The pupils of the eyes are fixed centrally, dilated and do not react to light. This test involves shining a light directly into the pupils and establishing that they do not contract.

5. No reaction to painful stimuli: typically, the patient's breast bone is vigorously rubbed with the knuckles for about thirty seconds to determine if there is a reaction to pain. Other painful stimuli, such as pinching may be used instead of the 'sternal rub'.

If a patient passes all five tests, the body may be conveyed to the mortuary and a death certificate written.

There is ample evidence to indicate that doctors and other medical personnel make mistakes in diagnosing death. 'The woman who died three times', and who was the subject of a one hour TV documentary in 2000, is the most dramatic indication of these occasional lapses. By the age of 65, Allison Burchell of Horsham, Sussex had been pronounced dead on no less than three occasions. In 1952 when she was 17 years old she 'died' for the first time. She collapsed in a cinema and was taken to hospital where she was pronounced dead. However, though her body was totally paralysed, she was fully conscious and could hear everything the nurses said to one another as they prepared her body and eventually wheeled her into the mortuary. She recovered after about half an hour among the dead. Months of tests followed and she was finally diagnosed as suffering from severe narcolepsy. The symptoms of this disease include an irresistible urge to fall asleep and cataplexy. Extreme cataplexy can lead to sudden loss of muscle control and short term paralysis. The condition may leave a patient totally paralysed, yet fully conscious and able to hear everything that's happening. The second attack occurred a few years later. Again she woke up in a mortuary, surrounded by dead bodies. The third attack occurred in Melbourne in the mid-seventies after she had relocated to Australia. Paramedics pronounced her dead and only the determined intervention of her fifteen year old son prevented the hospital authorities from placing her body in an airtight refrigerated unit.

Reports of people waking up in body bags and mortuaries regularly feature in newspapers. A typical case was that of a 77 year old Brooklyn woman who was pronounced dead by a New York ambulance crew in February 2002 after she had been found unconscious on her bathroom floor. The ambulance paramedics left and a police forensic officer arrived two hours later only to discover that the woman was still alive. She was brought to hospital but died a few hours later. An enquiry was ordered but the whole affair merited no more than a few lines in the press.

This kind of misdiagnosis would be much more common but for the fact that in the case of an unexpected death or collapse, medical help is normally summoned and efforts at resuscitation routinely carried out, unless the patient displays unequivocal signs of death, such as rigor mortis, putrefaction, decapitation, or massive cranial and cerebral destruction. This kind of inter-vention is a relatively new development.

## CARDIO-PULMONARY RESUSCITATION (CPR)

Up to the late 1950s, when the heart stopped beating and breath-ing ceased, it was generally agreed that the person was dead. Consequently, heart attack, drowning and accident victims who lacked these vital signs were given no treatment. Since the sec-ond half of the twentieth century, however, interventions have been developed which have saved people from certain death by artificially maintaining respiration and heartbeat. These tech-niques do not bring the dead back to life, rather, they prevent the dying process from advancing to an irreversible stage. Unless resuscitation is carried out within minutes of collapse – fifteen minutes being the outer range – the victim will have sustained serious and irreversible brain damage.

The development of procedures to keep the heart and lungs working by external means started with heart massage in the early 1950s. In a desperate attempt to save a life, a surgeon might occasionally open the chest of a heart attack victim and squeeze the heart in order to maintain the circulation of the blood. This radical procedure demonstrated that blood supply to the brain could be sustained by artificial means after the heart had stopped. Later it was discovered that a small amount of arti-ficial circulation could be achieved without surgery by simply applying rhythmic external chest compression.

Two US doctors are credited with pioneering modern resusci-tation techniques. Dr James Elam proved that exhaled air from one person is sufficient to adequately oxygenate the system of another. With Dr Peter Safar he went on to develop mouth-to-mouth artificial respiration, now generally known as 'rescue breathing'. The US military endorsed the technique by adopt-ing it to revive unresponsive victims. In 1960, mouth-to-mouth and chest compression were combined to form a procedure called cardio-pulmonary resuscitation (CPR). In 1972 Leonard Cobb held the world's first mass citizen training in CPR in Seattle, Washington. He helped train over 100,000 people in this technique. CPR now forms an important part of basic first aid training and is widely practiced throughout the world.

CPR gives people in cardiac arrest a chance of survival. However, it is not as effective as people are led to believe. A survey of CPR in TV dramas indicated that the rate of survival was about 75 percent. In the real world, the chances range from zero to about five percent. However, since the 1990s the widespread availability and use of defibrillators have increased the chances of survival. These devices use an electric shock to stop fibrillation of the heart – the heart twitching ineffectively –in the hope that it will restart with rhythmic contractions.

Resuscitation procedures continue to develop and become even more sophisticated. The term 'chain of survival' is often used these days in relation to emergency procedures for dealing with sudden cardiac arrest. There are four links in a chain which involves everybody from casual bystanders to highly trained paramedics. Early access is the first link and it depends on a bystander having enough initiative to make an emergency call. The second link, early CPR, envisages a bystander or family member giving CPR to the patient within two minutes. Early defibrillation is the third, and probably the most important link. CPR alone cannot fully resuscitate a person suffering from sudden cardiac arrest, whereas an electric shock to the heart can restore a normal heartbeat. If CPR and defibrillation can be provided in the first eight minutes, the chances of survival are about one in five. If paramedics arrive within eight minutes to administer advanced cardiac treatment – the fourth link – the chances of survival increase to more than 40 percent.

INTENSIVE CARE
A person who arrives in hospital in cardio-pulmonary failure,

usually ends up in an intensive care unit, where a sophisticated array of machinery takes over vital functions which the body can no longer manage for itself. The most important part of the life support apparatus is the ventilator, also known as a respirator, which breathes for the patient.

These machines came into general use in the 1950s during the polio epidemic. This disease caused paralysis in various parts of the body. Sometimes the muscles of the chest and diaphragm which control breathing were affected. A patient afflicted in this way required the use of a ventilator to survive. The so called 'iron lung' was a life-saver for such people as it had the capacity to take over the breathing function. As large as a small motorcar, the early ventilators almost entirely enclosed the patient, with only the head protruding beyond its confines. It worked on a very simple principal. By forming a perfect seal between the patient's neck and the ventilator, the patient's body could be subjected to variable air pressure. By pumping air out of the iron lung, the pressure was lowered and the patient's chest expanded, thus drawing air in through the nose and mouth quite naturally. Pumping air into the ventilator reversed the process, forcing the chest down and causing the patient to exhale. Modern ventilators carry out the same function, but work on a different principle which does not require the body to be encased. Patients are 'intubated', that is, a tube is inserted in the windpipe, and oxygen enriched air is forced into the lungs. These devices are compact and very sophisticated.

Intensive care is very expensive. It has been estimated that it accounts for 20 percent of all hospital costs in the United States. In Britain it costs three to five times more to keep a patient in an intensive care unit compared to the cost of maintaining a patient in a general ward. The introduction of new technologies means that costs are escalating. Furthermore, the number of intensive care beds available is never sufficient to meet demand, and that situation is likely to get worse. In the US the total number of intensive care beds is dropping by about one percent per year because of the prohibitive expense of staffing and running such units.

The massive expenditure has produced miraculous results from time to time. Many cases have been reported of hypothermic patients, exhibiting all the clinical signs of death, who have fully recovered after intensive medical treatment. A child who was submerged in water for 66 minutes and whose initial core temperature was 15.2 degrees Celsius – normal temperature is 36.4 C – was restored to full health. The case of a female skier whose temperature dropped to 13.7 C when she was trapped beneath ice for over an hour, was reported in the British medical journal the *Lancet*. She was ventilated with oxygen and given CPR during a one-hour flight to hospital. There, she was warmed up using cardiopulmonary bypass. This allows the blood to be circulated and re-warmed outside the body by a machine that temporarily takes over the functions of the heart and lungs. After 60 days intensive care and further rehabilitation she also fully recovered. The only lasting effects were a tingling in her hands.

A person brought into an intensive care unit who fails to respond quickly to cutting edge therapies and who, at the same time, continues to hang on to life by a thread, presents the hospital authorities, and society as a whole, with one of the most difficult problems that can be encountered. Removing an unconscious, ventilator-dependent patient from intensive care is likely to result in death. Keeping such a patient on life support is very expensive and may deprive more responsive patients of benefiting from life-saving treatments. Finance, the competing claims of patients and their families, moral and philosophical issues are all relevant considerations in what are literally life and death judgements for the intensive care doctors.

# Organ Transplantation & Redefinition of Death

Throughout the 1960s, many deeply unconscious patients suffering from brain trauma as a result of head injury, haemorrhage or disease existed in a kind of limbo, neither alive nor dead, waiting in intensive care units for human thought to catch up with medical science. There appeared to be no easy answer to this doctors' dilemma. Unplugging the patient meant certain death; maintaining treatment seemed merely to extend the dying process to unconscionable lengths. The work of a South African surgeon finally provided the stimulus to solve the problem.

FIRST HEART TRANSPLANT OPERATIONS
Dr Christiaan Barnard performed the first two human heart transplant operations, in Groote Schuur Hospital, Capetown, within a two week period in December of 1967. The first patient died within 18 days, the second, Dr Philip Blaiberg, survived for 18 months. The South African surgeon became an international superstar overnight and the then pariah state of South Africa did its utmost to benefit from his reflected glory.

Newspapers reacted very positively to the story, even allowing themselves to be conned into publishing exaggerated accounts of the second heart recipient's state of health. The press reported that Dr Blaiberg was able to resume sexual relations with his wife shortly after the operation. A widely published syndicated photograph depicted Blaiberg lying in the sea, happily splashing in the waves. Later it was reliably reported that Blaiberg had to be carried into the water for the photograph and quickly rescued by his entourage immediately afterwards as he was in imminent danger of drowning.

The press failed to pick up on the real story: Dr Barnard had removed the beating heart of the donor patient who, according to the accepted definition of death at that time, was still alive, to benefit the transplant patient. Dr Raymond Hoffenberg was the doctor under whose care the heart 'donor', a young man who had suffered a severe brain haemorrhage, had been admitted to the Groote Schuur Hospital. On the occasion of Dr Barnard's death in September 2001, Dr Hoffenberg recalled, in an article in *The British Medical Journal*, the pressure he was put under to pronounce the young man dead: 'Any misgivings I might have felt about declaring someone dead while his heart was still beating were confounded by the thought that hesitation on my part...might be construed as an attempt to undermine the prestige that Barnard's exploit had conferred on the country'. He still hesitated, however, because his patient had a few neurological reflexes. He went home, returned a couple of hours later, still found the reflexes, and declined to pronounce him dead. At this stage he was asked by a member of the transplant team: 'what sort of heart are you going to give us?' The following morning, because he could no longer elicit any reflexes, he pronounced the patient dead and the operation went ahead.

NEW DEFINITIONS OF DEATH
In 1967, the concept of brain death did not exist. Death was still defined as the irreversible cessation of circulatory and respiratory functions. Because heart transplant operations, for optimum results, require that the donor heart be removed while still beating, the medical profession came under pressure to agree on a new definition of death. Transplants could not go ahead within the confines of the old concept of death without risking a charge of homicide. The transplant predicament added greater urgency to finding an acceptable solution to the problem of how to deal with profoundly unconscious patients who were being kept alive in hospitals, almost indefinitely, by the use of ventilators and other intensive care interventions. Nothing less radical than an updated concept of death could solve the problems. A new definition of death could empower doctors to disconnect

hopeless cases from life support and permit the legal removal of organs for transplantation. The benefits to both types of patients and their families were obvious.

In September 1968, less than a year after Dr Barnard's first two heart transplants, 'the *ad hoc* committee of Harvard Medical School' issued a report on the appropriate treatment of the totally unresponsive patient. The committee members agreed that life support could be withdrawn from patients diagnosed with 'irreversible coma' or 'brain death'. The committee stated that this condition was characterised by: absence of spontaneous respiration and all spontaneous muscular movements; total unawareness to external stimuli; no response to painful stimuli; fixed, dilated pupils; lack of eye movement even when hit or turned, lack of response to noxious stimuli; absence of tendon reflexes. In addition to these criteria it was recommended that the brain should be tested for electrical activity by means of an electroencephalograph (EEG) before arriving at a diagnosis of brain death. If the tracings produced by this device were flat, indicating no electrical activity, it could be taken as an additional indication of brain death. The committee cautioned that drug intoxication and hypothermia, which can cause similar but reversible symptoms, should be eliminated as causes of the patient's condition. The committee stated that, with appropriate consent, the organs of a brain dead patient could be removed for transplantation.

A legal opinion accompanying the report advised that brain dead patients should be pronounced dead before organ removal was carried out.

In the United States, a special task force called a President's Commission may be established from time to time by the President to study and report on an important area of public interest. Such a committee, called the 'President's Commission for the Study of Ethical Problems in Medicine and Biomedical and Behavioral Research', was set up with a brief to examine the new concept of death. The Commission defined death in 1981 as: either the irreversible cessation of circulatory and respiratory functions or irreversible cessation of all functions of the entire brain. The concept of 'brain death' now forms the basis of the Uniform Determination of Death Act which has been enacted by almost all US states and has been endorsed by the American Bar Association.

The medical and legal professions throughout most of the world followed the leadership of the US in accepting the concept of brain death. Some countries accepted the American model. In Britain, however, the definition of brain death, as the complete and irreversible loss of function of the brain stem, is significantly different. Anatomically and functionally, the human brain consists of three main parts: the cerebrum which sustains consciousness, memory and higher mental functions; the cerebellum which is crucial to muscle control; and the brain stem which mediates all communication between brain and body, and manages respiration and various reflex actions. Whereas in the US, continued electrical activity in the cerebrum or cerebellum has to be taken into account before brain death can be diagnosed, in Britain, any such residual activity is discounted. The crucial importance of the brain stem is that it controls respiration. If it irreversibly loses its capacity to function, spontaneous respiration becomes impossible and the patient either dies or becomes ventilator-dependent.

The heart is not controlled by the brain. It functions independently. If it is continuously supplied with oxygenated blood, it continues to beat even after total brainstem destruction. The heart of a brain dead patient normally stops naturally after a few days, even if the patient is ventilated. The period between the cessation of spontaneous respiration and the cessation of heartbeat is usually between two and ten days, but may last considerably longer. A brain dead pregnant woman was kept alive on a ventilator for more than two months and gave birth, by

Caesarian section, to a live baby. The heart of another brain dead person continued to beat for more than fourteen years.

## COMA AND PERSISTENT VEGETATIVE STATE

In the mind of the general public, other conditions are often mistakenly equated with brain death, particularly coma and persistent vegetative state. However, these conditions are quite different. A coma is a profound state of unconsciousness. The term comes from the Greek word for sleep. A person in a coma cannot be awakened, does not respond to pain, does not have sleep-wake cycles, but may be able to breathe spontaneously. Coma may result from a variety of causes including drug or alcohol overdose, diabetes, haemorrhage or brain trauma. Coma generally lasts a few days to a few weeks, but rarely more than four weeks. Coma patients tend to recover, gradually regaining consciousness, or to deteriorate to a vegetative state, or to die.

A vegetative state sometimes follows a coma. This has been described as a state of wakefulness without detectable awareness. Patients in this condition exhibit sleep-wake cycles. They may open their eyes, grind their teeth, swallow, smile, shed tears, grunt, moan, laugh, or scream without any external cause. Spontaneous movements may also occur. The higher powers of the brain appear to be absent, but the functions of the brainstem, including the capacity to breathe spontaneously are retained. Patients in a vegetative state are unresponsive to external stimuli except, possibly, pain.

Coma patients who do not regain consciousness within 30 days are said to be in a persistent vegetative state (PVS). Even at this point, there is still a 50 percent chance of recovery within six months. After that, the likelihood of regaining consciousness becomes more remote. People have survived in this wakeful unconscious state for more than 15 years. Some doctors believe that a persistent vegetative state is an irreversible condition, and that those who appear to recover from it were not suffering from it in the first place! Catch-22 logic is unassailable.

## DIAGNOSING BRAIN DEATH

A deep and long lasting coma is not brain death. A persistent vegetative state is not brain death. Those charged with diagnosing brain death must ensure that patients suffering from conditions which mimic brain death are not misdiagnosed.

Doctors begin, therefore, by trying to ascertain whether the patient's unresponsive condition is due to factors such as the effects of a drug or alcohol overdose, paralysing drugs, hypothermia, or a neurological condition. If those factors can be ruled out, and the actual cause of unconsciousness can be ascertained, tests follow to determine whether brain-stem reflexes are present. The tests vary from country to country but usually include: checking that the pupils stay in midposition and do not react to bright light; that the eyes do not blink when the cornea is touched with a swab; that the eyes do not rotate in the socket when the head is moved from side to side or up and down; that the eyes do not move when ice water is placed in the ear canal; that the patient does not cough or gag when a suction tube is placed deep into the breathing tube. All of those functions are controlled by the brain-stem and their absence indicates loss of brain-stem function.

The brain-stem also controls breathing, but not in the way that one might imagine. Breathing is not stimulated by low levels of oxygen in the blood. The breathing reflex is activated by high levels of carbon dioxide. The body's anxiety to rid itself of carbon dioxide is the reason why it is unpleasant to hold one's breath. No discomfort is experienced as a result of oxygen deprivation, though it inevitably leads to unconsciousness and death. The apnoea test is used to determine whether the patient is capable of breathing spontaneously, which would indicate continued life in the brain-stem. The test requires the removal of the patient from the ventilator for a period of about ten minutes. Before this is done, measures are taken to ensure that there is an ample supply of oxygen in the patient's blood. After a few non-breathing minutes, carbon dioxide builds up and spontaneous respiration would commence in the case of a functioning brain-stem. While the test is in progress, the increasing levels of carbon dioxide in the blood are measured. If the patient does not breathe spontaneously after carbon dioxide concentrations reach a certain level, then the patient is deemed to have failed the apnoea test. Apnoea testing is somewhat controversial because it is a dangerous procedure and is often conducted without adequate precautions. Some doctors suggest that it is tantamount to testing a patient to death, and point out that an apnoea test cannot benefit a patient in any way.

Other additional tests may also be carried out. Cerebral angiography involves the injection of a harmless radioactive substance into the patient's blood stream and the use of a scanner to track the circulation of the blood throughout the body. In brain-dead patients, scanning will reveal an abrupt cut off of circulation below the base of the brain with no visible fluid draining away. This is a very strong indication of brain death. In many countries an electroencephalogram (EEG) test is used to confirm brain death. Electrodes are attached to the patient's head and recordings are taken of any electrical activity for a period of about 30 minutes. A flat EEG is taken as an indication of brain death.

Tests are repeated between six to twenty-four hours later. The first set of tests establish the cessation of brain function, the second set, if still negative, indicate irreversibility. However, misdiagnosis of brain death is possible. Apart from hypothermia and intoxication, other conditions also closely mimic the brain death, notably Guillain-Barré syndrome and locked-in syndrome.

Guillain-Barré syndrome is a disorder in which the body's

immune system attacks the nervous system. The symptoms of the disorder, which may develop in the course of a few hours, involve progressive muscular weakness culminating in almost total paralysis. The patient may have to be put on a respirator to aid breathing. Most patients recover from even the most severe attacks of this condition. *The Indian Journal of Critical Care Medicine* reported in 2003 the case of a 14 year old boy who was hospitalised with the syndrome. His condition rapidly deteriorated and he was put on a ventilator. After five days his pupils became fixed and dilated, all brain-stem reflexes were absent and the patient met the clinical criteria for brain-stem death. Luckily, an EEG test was performed and it picked up electrical activity in his brain. Life support measures were continued and five and a half months later the boy was discharged from hospital.

Locked-in syndrome is a rare neurological ailment involving complete paralysis of voluntary muscles throughout the body, apart from those that control eye movements. It may result from various conditions including brain injury, diseases of the circulatory system and medication overdose. People who suffer from this malady are conscious, with the main powers of the mind intact, such as the ability to think and reason, but they are without the powers of speech and movement. The capacity to move the eyes makes some form of communication possible. There is no cure for locked-in syndrome, and the chances of even limited recovery are not good.

If the doctors are satisfied that brain death has occurred, the ventilator may be switched. Death in the more conventional sense occurs soon afterwards. The heart is starved of oxygen and stops. All vital signs disappear after a few minutes.

ALL THE DEAD LIE DOWN?

Before the ventilator is switched off, the question of organ donation is usually discussed with the family of the deceased. Even if a patient has made clear an intention of donating organs after death, in practice that decision is left up to the next of kin. This state of affairs reflects the change in status brought about by death: a cadaver does not have rights under the law. However, it is unusual for the family to refuse organ donation if the patient had spoken about a desire to donate organs or had signed an organ donation card. More often than not, patients on life support systems will have made no decisions in this regard and it is left entirely up to the family to determine what to do.

If the next of kin agrees to organ donation, the ventilator is left on and other life support systems are not removed. The ventilator ensures that the body continues to be supplied with oxygenated blood. This allows the heart to continue to beat spontaneously and all the other bodily systems to function. Life support continues until the organs have been removed, after which the ventilator is switched off, and death in the conventional sense follows.

The terms 'organ harvesting' and 'organ retrieval' are generally used to describe the removal of organs from brain dead patients for purposes of transplantation. Neither of the terms is truly descriptive of the process. 'Harvesting' suggests the joyful gathering in of a ripened crop – hardly applicable in this context. Indeed, one might imagine the harvester sharing the spoils with the reaper, that is the Grim Reaper. 'Retrieval' is even less appropriate. It suggests getting something back that had been lost, or rescuing or saving something. Both terms seem to cut the deceased person, the donor, out of the picture, the person to whom the organs inalienably belong. Organ removal or organ donation seem to be the most accurate and fair terms to use.

The reason why organ removal takes place while the heart is still beating was succinctly explained by US transplant surgeon Pauline W. Chen, in an article entitled 'Dead Enough?: The Paradox of Brain Death', published in *The Virginia Quarterly Review* in 2005. She states: 'Whether you are transplanting a liver or a heart or a kidney or a pancreas, the better the donor is, the better your patient's outcome will be. And the very best of those donors is one who, when under the knife, is as close to alive as possible'. In the same article she draws attention to the instinctive reaction to this procedure: 'I have to admit that despite all I know about brain death, I still have my moments of uncertainty. More than once, when I have pulled my scalpel across the warm, pliable skin of a donor and seen the exuberant reds of well-oxygenated bleeding...' Her misgivings were not based on a fear that the patients were not 'dead enough', she regretted 'having to keep them so alive'.

It is easy to feel repugnance at the thought of removing organs from a warm, pink, heart beating donor because it is so difficult to accept that such a donor is actually dead. Feelings of this nature may lead one to reject organ donation. However, the matter is too important to be determined by instinct. It is worthy of very serious consideration. Organ donation saves many lives every year. Donors can also give a new lease of life to people whose existence is severely restricted by organ damage. A single donor can donate a heart, lungs, two kidneys, pancreas, liver, small bowel, two corneas, bone, skin and tendons. The kidneys can take two people off dialysis vastly improving their quality of life; the corneas can restore sight to two blind people; new surgical techniques can split a liver thus saving two lives; donated skin has helped people with severe burns; and bone is used in orthopaedic surgery. A single donor can help more than 20 people. It is difficult to argue against a procedure that saves so many lives and rescues so many people from misery. On the other hand, nobody can be expected to volunteer for organ donation, or to give permission for the removal of organs from the body of a relative, unless they can be fully assured that the procedure takes place only after the body is totally and irreversibly incapable of any level of consciousness.

How sure can we be that those diagnosed as brain dead are

actually dead? The first point to be made in this regard is that since the brain is the only part that's dead, the rest of the body manifests multiple signs of life. The heart beats spontaneously and without any mechanical assistance. The other organs, such as the liver, lungs and kidneys all carry out their biological functions. The body may also remain capable of some spontaneous movements, including a slow turning of the head to one side, movements of toes, facial twitching and various reflexes. The most dramatic movement is the so called 'Lazarus reflex'. This rarely seen reflex involves an apparent attempt by the body to flex at the waist, making it seem to rise. Sometimes the arms may be raised independently or together. These movements, if they occur, may be observed during the apnoea test, and when the abdominal incision is made for the removal of organs. It is generally accepted by the medical profession that these are reflexes generated by the spinal cord.

Brain dead patients may be anaesthetised while their organs are being removed. This fact is not generally known. Even those who volunteer for organ donation and those who permit organs of deceased relatives to be removed may not be made aware of this information. It is logical to assume that the purpose of the anaesthesia is to prevent the brain dead from suffering during the surgical procedure, an assumption that suggests that the brain dead are not quite numb. The following extract is from a submission to an internet discussion forum on organ donation. It is self-explanatory:

'Our son was determined to be brain dead in 1993... We donated [his] organs in an attempt to derive something good from a terrible situation. We were told that [he] was a perfect candidate for major organ donation. His brain stem had been crushed in an accident but he had no other injuries... the patient is kept alive on a ventilator until all of the organs have been removed...A few years later there was a dispute in England among anaesthesiologists because of the reaction of brain dead patients during the organ retrieval process. Apparently if no anaesthetic is used patients react to the pain of incisions by trying to move away from the scalpel. At the moment the scalpel cuts, the patient's blood pressure and heartbeat increase dramatically as well. This is well documented medically but not commonly known by the public. We certainly were never informed of it. Had we been informed we would never have consented to organ retrieval and would have let our son die naturally. I called the organ retrieval team in BC [British Columbia, Canada] to see if they had used any anaesthetic during the procedures on our son. I was told that they do not because the patient would not be considered brain dead if anaesthetic were necessary. The procedure would be considered euthanasia, which is illegal under Canadian Law. They acknowledged the fact that patients do react during the procedure but likened the movement to that of a chicken when its head has been cut off. You can imagine how this analogy was received. As a parent, I feel like I have unwittingly subjected my son to unknown pain. I feel that we were deliberately mislead.'

While it is close to certain that the surgeon's scalpel caused no pain to the brain dead young man, it is indisputable that the withholding of information from his mother caused that woman incalculable suffering. Now, it would be explained to her that muscle paralysing agents may be used to suppress reflex movements, and that some form of anaesthesia could be used to control the sudden rise in blood pressure and the rapid heart rate that accompany the trauma of surgery. Peter Hutton, president of the Royal College of Anaesthetists and Maldwyn Morgan, president of the Association of Anaesthetists of Great Britain and Ireland issued a joint statement in 2000 giving an assurance that brain-dead donors could not feel pain during operations to remove their organs for transplants: 'Anaesthetic drugs suppress unconscious physiological reflexes [such as blood pressure changes and heart rates] and can be used in this way during organ removal procedures ... Anaesthetic drugs are not needed to suppress consciousness ... the patient is already in a deep coma'.

## ELECTIVE VENTILATION: A BRIDGE TOO FAR

A practice carried out in the city of Exeter, Devon to increase the supply of organs for transplantation was eventually found to be illegal under British law. Patients suffering from devastating strokes and rendered deeply comatose by their condition are known to have an extremely low chance of survival and they eventually succumb to brain death. With the permission of the family, such patients were routinely transferred to intensive care units shortly before death and ventilated. When brain death occurred, and spontaneous breathing would have ceased, the ventilator ensured that the system continued to be oxygenated, thus preserving the organs. This procedure ensured that the organs remained suitable for transplantation and allowed sufficient time to remove them. Elective ventilation resulted in a 100 percent increase in organ availability.

However, the procedure was deemed not to be in the interest of the dying patients. Its only purpose was to secure transplantable organs. It also carried with it a small risk that patients who would otherwise have died would survive in a persistent vegetative state. Even with the consent of the patient's family, it was decided that elective ventilation should be discontinued. The only thing that could justify exposing patients to a risk that could have no benefit for themselves, is their previously obtained explicit consent. In 1994, elective ventilation was declared to constitute battery and was declared unlawful.

## WHAT'S A BODY TO DO?

The concept of brain death slipped into most countries without fanfare and with little or no public discussion on the matter. Whatever controversy was generated by the issue was confined, for the most part, to the medical profession. In countries where brain death became a topic of public controversy, notably Germany, Denmark and Japan, there tended to be strong objections to it, with a sizeable proportion of the population rejecting the concept.

A vigorous public debate on brain death was carried on in Japan for decades. It was started by a botched heart transplant operation carried out in 1968. The topic became so fraught that the second Japanese heart transplant did not take place until 1999, 31 years after the first. Over 100 books were written on brain death, to feed the public interest, two of them by well known Japanese journalists. Michi Nakajima wrote *Invisible Death* in which she rejected the idea of brain death. She maintained that family members could not accept that a relative manifesting many signs of life was not alive; that the idea was in conflict with ordinary human intuition. Takashi Tachibana's *Brain Death* insisted that brain death tests could not test the actual death of brain cells, pointing out that an EEG cannot detect electrical activity in cells that are deep within the brain.

In line with most countries, Japan redefined death to facilitate organ donation. However, the law in Japan clearly reflects the passionate and protracted public debate that had preceded the legislation. The law does not provide a uniform definition of death. It allows people to choose between traditional death and brain death. A person who wants to be an organ donor must record that intention while still of sound mind. That person will then be considered dead if brain death is diagnosed. A person who has not recorded an intention to be an organ donor, even if diagnosed as brain dead, is not considered to be dead until the heart stops beating. In addition, consent of the patient's family is required in order to remove organs and in order for brain death to be accepted as death.

An extra protection accorded to brain injured Japanese is that, in the initial testing for brain death, the apnoea test is excluded.

This recognises the fact that, turning off a ventilator for up to 10 minutes to see if spontaneous breathing starts, may be detrimental to the patient's health. If the patient is diagnosed as brain dead by the initial tests, and if the patient had expressed in writing a desire to be an organ donor, and if the patient's family are in agreement with the decision, then an apnoea test may be carried out. If brain death is then confirmed, organ removal may commence. Otherwise, the patient is not deemed to be dead until the heart stops beating and respiration ceases.

The general public in Japan are very familiar with the details of organ donation and their medico-legal system affords great protection to patients with serious brain injuries. However, many Japanese believe that the system is stacked against patients who require organs. Both the donor and the donor's family must agree to the removal of organs before it can take place. If the brain dead patient had not previously expressed in writing a willingness to be an organ donor, the consent of the family is not sufficient to allow organ removal. In contrast, in most countries, if the patient's wishes are not known and the family agree to organ donation, the procedure may go ahead.

Organ donation is a very complex area. A briefing document on the subject, published by the Royal College of General Practitioners for its members, concludes with the following statement:

'Potential donors and relatives of potential donors need a full and clear understanding of brain stem death, in particular, that the heart can continue to beat spontaneously in a brain stem dead person. Written information on these points could be provided as a reminder. [Potential donors] need to know how such persons are maintained clinically once they have been medically certified as brain stem dead, prior to donation. They need to be aware of the use of anaesthetic agents during organ retrieval, to the extent of full anaesthesia. If, in the light of solid information about the clinical circumstances of death confirmed by brain stem tests and with due assurances about the possibility of providing full-spectrum anaesthesia where requested, people are then happy to offer themselves as donors, then the ethical requirements for valid consent to be a donor are fulfilled'.

## OCKHAM'S RAZOR

In medieval philosophy, Ockham's razor was an important aid in finding the truth. The principle is called after William of Ockham, a thirteenth century theologian, who was its most accomplished exponent. Simply put, Ockham's razor is the belief that the explanation requiring the fewest assumptions is most likely to be correct, or to put it another way, the simplest explanation for any phenomenon is likely to be more accurate than the complicated explanation. To conclude that a brain dead patient is dead, one has to accept a new definition of death, which includes the concept that the presence of vital signs does not indicate the presence of life. Ockham's razor would suggest that if there is life in the body, the body is alive.

A significant proportion of Japanese people would agree with this. They believe that the essence of a human being exists in the body as well as in the mind. For them, the brain dead are still alive. Modern Western thought equates self awareness with humanity and death with the lack of a capacity for consciousness, thus permitting no conclusion other than that the brain dead are really dead. Take your pick.

# 6. It's Your Funeral

Shortly after a death has taken place, the family of the deceased appoint an undertaker, who arranges for the collection of the body from the home, hospital or morgue, and its delivery to the funeral home. Details of the funeral must then be worked out by the family in conjunction with the undertaker. A decision must be made on whether to embalm the body, a coffin must be selected, and the method of final disposal decided upon – usually either cremation or burial – though other options exist.

## Embalming and Body Preparation

When the remains arrive at the undertaker's premises, typically, they are laid out on a stainless steel or porcelain embalming table, very similar to an autopsy table. All clothing is removed and the body is cleaned by sponging with a disinfectant spray. The effects of rigor mortis are counteracted by flexing, bending and massaging the limbs. When loose enough, the legs are extended and the arms placed by the sides.

Massage cream is worked into the face and hands to keep them soft and pliable. The nose is plugged with cotton, and cotton or gauze is placed in the throat to absorb fluids. The mouth is closed with sutures or wire, taking care that the lips meet naturally. If the mouth is closed too tightly, the skin between the nose and upper lip puckers and produces an unpleasant scowl. The lips and eyelids may be glued to keep them closed in a suitable expression. After that, the body is normally embalmed.

Embalming is a measure which retards the decomposition process, preventing the body from deteriorating in appearance and emitting offensive odours during the funeral period. If the body has not been stabilised in this way, undertakers are very reluctant to allow viewing, for very understandable reasons. In North America, undertakers make it quite clear that no embalming means no viewing. There, embalming is the norm and is known to be the norm. In other countries, things are not so clear-cut. In Ireland, most bodies are also embalmed – perhaps nine out of ten – but very few people are aware of that fact and even fewer have any familiarity with what embalming involves.

In the early months of 2006, the Irish Association of Funeral Directors (IAFD) campaigned vigorously against a 'biocide directive', issued by the Environment Commissioner of the European Union, banning the use of formaldehyde, the most important chemical used in embalming. All members of the Irish parliament were lobbied by letter to oppose the measure. The letter included the following paragraph: 'The cessation of embalming would generally mean that viewing in funeral homes and private residences would cease as we know it. The problem posed by the uninhibited decomposition of deceased would necessitate enormous investment by health authorities in the provision of cold storage, while awaiting medical certification and availability of cemeteries and crematoria, particularly at weekends.' Curiously, the IAFD managed to carry on its robust pro-embalming campaign, without a single journalist asking questions about the details of the process and the extent to which it is practiced.

Embalming is a two part process. First, arterial embalming removes the blood from the circulatory system and replaces it with a mixture of formaldehyde and water. A small incision is made on the right side of the lower neck to access the carotid artery and the jugular vein, two of the largest blood vessels in the body. Some embalmers have a preference for the femoral arteries and veins located in the thighs rather than of those on the neck. Incisions are made in both vessels and a tube is inserted into each. The carotid artery is then connected to a fluid pump, while the tube in the jugular vein acts as a drain. Two or three gallons of fluid are then pumped into the body, flushing out all the blood in the circulatory system and replacing it with the chemical which is a combination disinfectant and preservative. If there are blood clots or other blockages in the system, it may be necessary to pump fluids into other sites as well as the main neck artery. The embalmer may easily chart the progress of the operation because the fluid normally has a pinkish dye added to it. As it courses through the veins and arteries, the waxy white appearance of the corpse is gradually replaced by a healthy looking glow. The blood is allowed to flow down the drain, like the dirty water that was used to wash the corpse earlier. It poses no health risk.

Cavity embalming is the second part of the process. If an autopsy has been performed, the organs are immersed in embalming fluid and replaced in the body cavity, often surrounded by a preservative powder. Otherwise, the embalmer uses a surgical instrument called a trocar, which consists of a puncturing device inside a tube. Its purpose is the removal of fluids and gases from the abdominal and chest cavities. A small incision is made just above the navel, and the trocar, attached to a suction pump, is inserted. The mortician then punctures and

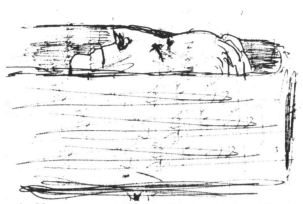

FIGURE 6: VIEWING THE BODY: PHOTOGRAPHING A BODY IN A FUNERAL PARLOUR WOULD BE REGARDED AS HIGHLY DISRESPECT-FUL; SKETCHING, A MORE TRADITIONAL ART, IS ACCEPTABLE. INTERESTINGLY, IN BRITISH AND IRISH COURTROOMS, THE SAME RULE APPLIES: PHOTOGRAPHY IS BANNED BUT SKETCHING IS PER-MISSIBLE. (DRAWING BY DIARMUID Ó LIATHAIN)

drains the stomach, bladder, large intestines and lungs and aspi-rates all fluids and gases. The trocar is then used to direct full strength formaldehyde solution into each organ. All incisions are then sutured closed, completing the process of embalming. The anus and vagina may be packed with cotton or gauze to pre-vent seepage. A close-fitting plastic pants may also be used for added security

The body is washed again, this time with cool water and ger-micidal solution to kill viruses and bacteria. Then close atten-tion is given to the parts of the body that will be on view. The fingernails are cleaned, and solvents are used to remove any stains on the remains. Special chemicals may be used to remove scaling on the hands and face. The hair may be washed before embalming, but hairdressing is usually done afterwards. Facial hair and any visible nose hair are removed from all bodies, including those of women and children who may have excess facial hair because of medications.

The corpse is then dressed up in the clothes supplied by the family. It is normal to use a full set of clothing, including underwear, socks or stockings, and sometime even shoes. Makeup is applied to face and hands, usually special mortuary cosmetics, though ordinary makeup may also be used.

Finally, the body is placed in a coffin or casket. The funeral director tries to pose both the head and hands in a life-like position for viewing by family, friends, colleagues, acquaintances and the inquisitive.

## Coffin and Casket

The coffin is normally the single most expensive funeral item. In the past, coffins have been made from wood, stone, metal, pottery and other materials and have been variously shaped. The traditional, six-sided wooden box, which broadens to accommodate the shoulders and tapers to the head and feet has gone out of fashion in the United States and been replaced by a coffin of rectangular design – generally known as a 'casket'. With its hinged lid and more roomy interior, usually elaborately lined with velvet, crepe or taffeta, it presents the deceased for viewing in an impressive manner

Choice of coffin is heavily influenced by whether the body is to be buried or cremated. It is hard to justify the purchase of anything other than a cheap combustible receptacle made from material such as fibreboard, pressed wood or cardboard, if the choice is cremation, as the coffin is always incinerated with the body. If the body is to be buried, however, choosing a coffin may require more consideration.

## *Cremation*

Cremation was being used as a method of disposing of human bodies more than five thousand years ago. Evidence of Bronze Age cremation (2500-1000 BC) has been found in sites as far apart as Hungary and Ireland; and Spain and Northern Italy. By 800 BC, it was the dominant mode of disposing of the dead in Greece. The Greeks were trend setters in the Classical world, and the Romans followed their lead. Incineration became the preferred option throughout most of the Roman Empire, for a period of four centuries. Some individuals and groups, however, still opted for burial. The Jews in particular never burned their dead. Nor did the adherents of the emerging Christian sect, which grew out of the Jewish tradition.

When the emperor Constantine the Great introduced religious freedom throughout the Empire and later showed favour towards Christians, the new religion gained many more members and eventually went on to entirely replace paganism. The rapid rise of Christianity led to the equally rapid demise of cremation. By the fifth century, the practice of cremation had entirely ceased except in some areas remote from the civilisation of the time.

For fifteen hundred years, burial was almost the only method of body disposal in Europe. Rare exceptions include instances of mass incineration of bodies during plagues and epidemics. During an outbreak of the black death in 1656, for example, the bodies of 60,000 victims were burned in Naples in a single week. History has also recorded some bizarre individual cremations. The burning of the body of Romantic poet Percy Bysshe Shelley on a beach near Viareggio in Italy in 1822 fits into this category.

Shelley was drowned with two others when his schooner sank in a storm. His body was washed ashore after a few days and it was in an advanced state of decomposition when discovered by

113

his friends. They arranged a do-it-yourself cremation on the beach. The chief organiser, Lord Trelawney, wrote a rather gruesome account of the event. Shelley's skull burst open and 'as the back of the head rested on the red-hot bottom bars of the furnace, the brains literally seethed, bubbled, and boiled as in a cauldron, for a very long time'. The entire body was consumed by fire except for some fragments of bones, the jaw and the skull. Trelawney managed to rescue Shelley's heart which was exposed when 'the corpse fell open'. Later, this was presented to Shelley's widow.

By its inclusion in Trelawny's *Recollections of the Last Days of Shelley and Bryon*, the event was given wide exposure. Shelley's fame and notoriety, and the presence at the ceremony of Lord Byron, one of the period's greatest celebrities, helped to fix the concept of cremation in the common mind as a wild, romantic reminder of a pagan era, rather than a practical way of disposing of bodies.

From the mid-nineteenth century doctors, scientists and social reformers, on both sides of the Atlantic, began to argue in favour of cremation. The suggested benefits over burial included fewer public health problems, lower amounts of pollution, more land for the living, and lower costs. Cremation would also prevent bodies from being stolen for use by medical schools, a possibility feared by many people at that time. Many municipal cemeteries were equipped with manned watchtowers to prevent the disinterment by night of freshly buried bodies by 'resurrection men'.

There were practical problems associated with cremation. The incineration of a human body would have to be done in a manner acceptable to the public. Even the most ardent supporters of cremation did not expect to see the smoke of funeral pyres rising from the towns and villages of the Western World. After years of experimentation, Professor Brunetti from Italy developed a dependable combustion chamber. It was displayed at the

Vienna Exposition in 1873. The solving of all technical difficulties led to the construction of the first crematoria. The first in North America was built in 1876 by Dr Julius LeMoyne in Washington, Pennsylvania. The first in Europe were built in 1878, one in Woking, England the other in Gotha, Germany. Legal difficulties, which were not sorted out until 1884, prevented the use of the English crematorium for five years after its completion.

From a standing start, the new method of body disposal made spectacular gains in a relatively short space of time. There were only three cremations in Britain in 1885, rising to 1,000 in 1912 and 10,000 in 1936. By 1968 cremation and burial were neck and neck. Today, cremation is the preferred option in Britain, where it follows approximately 70 percent of all deaths

The story in the USA indicates a similar steep rise in a short space of time. Currently six states have a cremation rate of over 50 percent: Arizona, Hawaii, Montana, Nevada, Oregon and Washington. The national rate is over 25 percent and rising. In Canada, about 45 percent of all deaths result in cremation.

There are three crematoria in the Republic of Ireland, all of them in Dublin. About 15 percent of funerals in Dublin terminate in cremation; in Ireland as a whole the cremation option is selected in about 5 percent of all deaths.

The cremation process has not changed much since its inception over a century ago. The body arrives in a coffin, rigid, leak-proof and made from combustible material. It is brought by trolley to the furnace and slid into the brick-lined, vaulted chamber, where it fits snugly. The drop-down furnace door is closed and the operator begins the procedure by switching on a fan to direct a strong stream of air through the chamber and up the chimney. This ensures a plentiful supply of oxygen when the combustion begins. Then various gas burners come on in sequence. The first one is to preheat the chamber to prevent cracking of the brick by a sudden and intense burst of heat; the ignition burner directs flames downwards from the roof to ignite the coffin; finally a powerful burner kicks in, directing a fierce blast of heat onto the body. The temperature of the furnace is maintained at between 900 and 1,000 degrees Celsius. There is much in the human body that is combustible and when an obese body ignites it can increase the temperature to 1,600 degrees.

Cremation time varies with the size and weight of the body. It can take from one to four hours to reduce a corpse to substances that can be neither burnt nor vaporised. The remains are allowed to cool down. Then they are removed from the furnace. A magnet is run over them to collect metallic objects such as nails and screws that may have formed part of the coffin, and items like surgical pins from the body. The 'cremains', as cremated remains are now generally called, consist almost entirely of bone fragments. They are pulverised and milled after which they take on the appearance of crushed sea shells. The average weight of cremains, for men is about seven and a half pounds, six pounds for women, and lesser amounts for children, depending on size. Infants may be entirely vaporised and leave no trace at all behind in the furnace. Generally speaking, the body is reduced to about five percent of its weight in a few hours. The cremains are placed in a container and made available for collection about a day after the body arrived in the crematorium.

## Burial

Whereas the cremation process does not vary much in the tens of thousands of crematoria worldwide, there are major differences in burial practices throughout the globe. Two recent exhumations, one in Cork City, Ireland, the other in Georgia, USA, illustrate contrasting styles of burial in the new and the old world.

When a judge decided that entitlement to a bitterly disputed inheritance could be resolved only by carrying out a number of DNA tests, permission had to be obtained to disinter two bodies: that of Ellen O'Regan, who had been buried in a Savannah cemetery for over sixty years, and the body of her alleged brother, Jeremiah, who had been buried in St Finbarr's cemetery in Cork. A DNA match would result in a serious reversal for the family who had been awarded the inheritance.

Ellen O'Regan's grave was easily located in St Bonaventure's cemetery. A mechanical digger excavated until its steel arm scraped on a hard, unyielding surface. Further clearing exposed a concrete box, or vault, deep in the grave. The cover was removed. Inside, the sixty year old casket was in pristine condition. When it was brought to the surface and opened, the body was found to be intact. It had been embalmed before burial and appeared to have been mummified over time, though some parts were damaged by water seepage. Two inches of femur were removed by a forensic anthropologist and the body was returned to the grave.

Jeremiah's grave was also easily located in the large municipal cemetery in Cork, but after that, nothing else was easy. Over the years, at least four other bodies had been buried in that single grave, at different intervals of time. Each of the coffins would have eventually collapsed, unable to support the great weight of soil piled on top of it. At each new burial, the remains of the existing occupants would have been disturbed. Bones may have been dredged up by the gravediggers and thrown back in, ending up in different positions to where they had previously lain. Contact with the soil would have helped the remains to decay quickly, especially as the bodies are unlikely to have been embalmed. Each time the grave had been dug anew, old coffin boards, if they had not rotted away, would have been removed and burned in order to make more room.

Though the dates and sequence of all the burials were known, it was not possible to distinguish who was who from the jumble of bones discovered when the grave was opened. The forensic anthropologist eventually took bone samples from three different femurs. DNA tests indicated no match between the two bodies.

Advertising in the US to promote graves and grave paraphernalia often suggests that the permanent preservation of the remains is both possible and desirable. Though it is illegal to make such claims explicitly, manufacturers regularly emphasise the strength and durability of their products, laying stress on factors like special seals on caskets to prevent the entry of air and water.

In Europe, corpses escaping their 'dust to dust' destiny is regarded as very undesirable. Indeed, European scientists are investigating how to speed up rather than slow down the decomposition process. In Germany, where over half a million people are buried in coffins annually, a strange phenomenon has been observed in recent years. To quote one German undertaker who put the matter succinctly: 'bodies that were put into the ground 30 years ago look like they went in last week'. The same thing is happening in other countries, including Austria and Switzerland.

In Europe, graves have always been shared or reused. Gravediggers reopen graves to bury new coffins in the expectation that coffins previously buried have collapsed and crumbled into dust, along with their occupants, a process expected to take eight to ten years. Now, about one third of the graves in Germany, those in which burials took place in the last thirty to forty years, are not yet reusable. Explanations offered for slow decomposition include a human diet high in preservatives, the wiping out of bacteria by pesticides and a build up of toxins in the soil from amalgams used in dental fillings, soil that is too dry, soil that is too wet.

## *Other Disposal Options*

Most bodies are destined for either cremation or burial, but there are other ways of disposing of human remains, including burial at sea, donation for dissection by medical students, and donation for research purposes. Some enterprising people have found a few novel ways of dealing with the problem.

BURIAL AT SEA

People with a maritime connection often request sea burial. There are two burial at sea sites in Britain, one off the Needles, Isle of Wight and the other between Hastings and Newhaven on the South Coast. Like many other jurisdictions, the British discourage the practice and allow it only under license and very stringent conditions. Bodies that have been subjected to an embalming process are not permitted to be buried at sea because the procedure substantially delays decomposition, thereby increasing the chance that the body may be returned to shore by tidal currents or caught in fishing gear, to the distress of all concerned.

The coffin is subjected to considerable stress when entering the sea and during its descent to the seabed and must be constructed in such a way as to ensure that it will withstand any likely impact and carry the body to its final resting place. About 400 pounds of ballast must be attached to the coffin and forty to fifty holes drilled in it to ensure that it quickly sinks to the seabed. A band of plastic or other durable material must be locked round the neck of the deceased, indelibly marked with a telephone number and reference number that would allow the remains to be positively identified should the need arise.

The United States Navy facilitates burial at sea requests from members of the uniformed services, retirees, veterans who were honourably discharged, and dependent family members. Cremains and properly prepared casketed remains are accepted on board naval vessels and disposed of at sea while the ship is deployed. Family members are not allowed to be present, since the ships are on active duty, but the commanding officer of the ship assigned to perform the burial at sea ceremony will notify the family of the date, time, longitude and latitude once the commital service has been performed.

BODY DONATION

Another method of disposing of one's remains, body donation, is open to everyone. Human bodies are in constant demand as essential teaching aids in medical schools and for purposes of scientific research. In many medical schools, student doctors start dissecting bodies in their first few months of training. An ample supply of corpses ensures that every student gets hands on experience. Shortages mean several students must share one body between them. Lack of first hand experience cannot be fully compensated for by textbooks, videos, demonstrations and other artificial substitutes. Human tissue is also needed by scientists working in the area of medical research and development.

In bygone centuries, bodies for dissection were in such short supply that the numbers had to be made up from the ranks of executed criminals and by corpses stolen from graveyards. Neither of those two sources are acceptable today, so the world of medicine must rely on volunteers. Most medical schools have their own body donation schemes which are designed to make this option as attractive as possible. Though the procedures differ from place to place, institutions try to ensure that normal funeral arrangements may be carried out before the body is taken away, and that the family incurs no additional expense. Also, an institution will normally arrange a burial or cremation of the remains when the body has fulfilled the function for which it was donated. Some independent agencies to which bodies may be donated act as suppliers of tissues, organs and whole bodies to medical schools and scientific laboratories. One such company, Science Care, states in its internet advertisement: 'The benefits to humankind are enormous. Medical training that involves the use of human tissues can advance the knowledge and skills of physicians and surgeons.'

TEACHING AID

A freelance writer in Milwaukee has made arrangements to donate her skeleton to the Milwaukee Institute of Art and Design. When she dies, her unembalmed body will be buried in a pine box, to speed up decomposition, and dug up five years later, by which time it will be skeletonised. The bones will then be delivered to Professor Fred Anapol, a forensic anthropologist who will articulate them, that is, string them together, with the assistance of some of his students as a class project. After that, she expects to spend about forty years in the classrooms of the Institute of Art and Design as an invaluable teaching aid. At the end of four or five decades, the bones will have become too dry and brittle for further use.

PLASTINATION BY VON HAGENS

If you would prefer to go into the entertainment business rather than education after your death, Professor Gunther von Hagens may be able to help. In January 1977 in the city of Heidelberg, he invented a 'plastination technique' which both preserves human tissue and enables the body to be displayed in any conceivable position. The process involves the replacement of bodily fluids with a plastic substance that solidifies. Initially, von Hagens regarded his discovery as a useful tool for medical research. When members of the general public saw his work – he put some of it on display at an open day in Heidelberg University – he was surprised by the level of interest.

Over the years he accumulated a large collection of corpses which he preserved in a variety of startling postures: standing

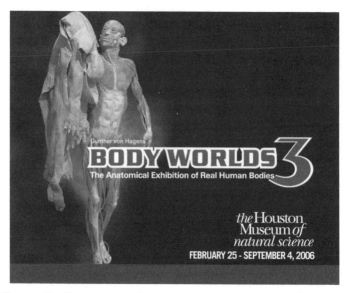

FIGURE 7: *BODYWORLDS 3* POSTER ADVERTISING ONE OF GUNTHER VON HAGENS' EXHIBITIONS OF 'PLASTINATED' HUMAN BODIES.

upright, sitting at tables, engaged in activities like playing chess, even riding bicycles. Most had cutaway sections. One side of the face might be intact, while the other side would be dissected to various depths, showing the muscles, blood vessels and bone structure underneath. Models with cutaway skulls exposing brains, dissected abdomens revealing all the organs, and flayed limbs with every muscle on view, proved irresistible to the public.

Eventually, von Hagens took to the road with his 'Bodyworlds' show. His first stop outside of Germany was Japan which he visited in 1996. He had to return in 1997 and 1998 to satisfy the public demand, and a final total of almost three million Japanese went to see the exhibition. Four other locations topped the million mark, including South Korea where over two million people went to see the plastinated bodies. When his work was on display in London in 2002 — more than half a million people went to view it in the first few months — he performed the first public autopsy in Britain for 170 years. Five hundred people paid to watch him remove the brain, kidneys, lungs, liver, spleen and heart from the body of a 72-year old man.

Professor von Hagens is looking for bodies. He claims that his specimens have all been donated and he offers a kind of afterlife in show business to anyone who would like to avail of the opportunity. He intends to be plastinated himself when he dies, along with any member of his family who wants to. So far, over 4,000 people have answered his call for volunteers.

# Funeral Arrangements

A number of factors influence choice of funeral arrangements. Local and family tradition is probably the strongest, especially since such tradition is often based on religious affiliation. Cost is another major consideration, followed by personal preference. If the views of the deceased are not known, the burden of all the decision making is left in the hands of the family.

IMPORTANCE OF RELIGIOUS AFFILIATION
The Jewish religion, with its multi-millennia tradition of burial, strongly discourages cremation. The Jews favour a simple ritual with closed wooden caskets and plain shrouds, endowing people with equality in death. Embalming is discouraged as an unnecessary interference with the body, because burial is meant to follow swiftly after death. For Jews, an additional argument against cremation relates to the Holocaust experience, when the bodies of millions of Jews were disposed of by fire in Nazi death camps. However, progressive Jews who opt for cremation

argue that it costs less than burial and is therefore better able to fulfil the goal of equality in death. If cremation is chosen, Jews are encouraged to bury the cremated remains as opposed to keeping them in the home or scattering them.

Islam is totally opposed to cremation. Burial is the prescribed method of disposing of the dead. As in the Jewish religion, immediate burial is considered to be desirable. The body is washed, wrapped in a shroud and buried, preferably without a coffin, facing Mecca. The use of markers and flowers on graves is not encouraged. Embalming has no place in Islamic funeral practice.

Christian churches follow the Jewish tradition in their preference for burial. With the passage of time, most Christian denominations have reconciled themselves to cremation, but the Roman Catholic Church has not yielded fully to the practice, though it is moving in that direction.

Roman Catholic opposition to cremation was never based on fears that it would prevent the resurrection of the body. Even the earliest Christians did not hold such literal and naïve beliefs. In fact, the Roman Catholic Church authorities have never claimed that cremation is directly opposed to any of the Church's fundamental teachings. Cremation was promoted initially by people who were regarded as the enemies of the church. Allied to that was the view that the destruction of a human body by fire was an act of gross disrespect. This stance led to an outright ban on cremation up as far as the 1960s. Today, the Church continues to prefer, and encourages its members, to bury the bodies of their departed loved ones. Catholics who opt for cremation may not be accorded the full funeral rites of the Church.

The Roman Catholic funeral ritual is in three parts. First, there is the vigil, in Ireland it is called the 'removal': a prayer service that takes place a short time after the death, typically in the funeral home. Next comes the most important part: the funeral mass. Finally, there is a commital ceremony at the graveside. Since cremated remains are not normally allowed into the Catholic churches for the funeral mass, the usual procedure is to cremate the body after the funeral mass, and to commit it to the grave when the remains become available. In some situations, a body may have to be cremated before the funeral mass. For example, if the death takes place a long distance from home, the cost of sending back a body rather than ashes could be prohibitive for some families. In such situations, it was usual to have the commital ceremony first and to have a memorial mass at a later stage.

It is generally accepted that this state of affairs is not satisfactory. The funeral rites take place in the wrong sequence, and the funeral mass, without the body or anything related to the body, is like *Hamlet* without the prince. Since the late 1990s, the Catholic Church has made further concessions in areas where cremation is popular, by permitting ashes, in certain situations, to be brought into the funeral mass and treated in the same way as the body of a deceased person. It is left up to the discretion of local bishops to determine in each case whether the particular circumstances merit this dispensation.

The Catholic Church also prescribes how cremated remains are to be treated. Scattering on the land, in the sea or from the air is frowned on. Human ashes should be placed in a 'worthy vessel' and treated with the same respect accorded to a body. When they are being moved, they should be carried or transported in a dignified manner. The final resting place should be in a cemetery, either buried in a grave or placed in a vault designed for cremated remains – called a 'columbarium'. It is also recommended that the place of entombment should be marked by some kind of memorial or gravestone.

Neither the Roman Catholic Church nor Christian churches in general are opposed to embalming. The last four popes, including John Paul II, were embalmed by the Signoracci family of undertakers in Rome with varying degrees of success. The remains of Pope John XXIII were embalmed in 1963 and when the body was exhumed in 2001 and transferred to St Peter's Basilica, the Italian daily newspaper, *Corrriere della Sera*, reported that it was in a remarkable state of preservation. The body of his successor, Pope Paul VI was only lightly embalmed on the instruction of the Vatican. After two days of lying in state, in the hot August of 1978, the body began to putrefy. It took on a greenish tinge and fans had to be installed in the basilica to disperse the smell.

The lying in state of an earlier Pope, Pius XII, in 1958 presented an even more extraordinary spectacle. His doctor refused to allow his body to be embalmed in the normal invasive manner, ordering instead a procedure which he believed to be an ancient Egyptian method. The experiment was a failure and the body decomposed significantly before burial. Accounts from the time describe his corpse turning emerald green and Swiss guards fainting from the smell. The claim by John Cornwell, in his 1999 book *Hitler's Pope*, that Pius's nose turned black and fell off, has been disputed.

THE COST FACTOR

Cost was always an important factor in deciding on funeral details and with escalating costs, it is becoming even more important. The findings of a British national survey of funeral costs, published in 2006, indicate that the prices in Britain had risen by 61 percent in the previous five years. The survey also clearly indicates the substantial difference in price between a burial and a cremation. The average cost of a funeral involving cremation is £1,954, while a funeral involving burial costs £3,307, making a burial almost 70 percent more expensive. The substantial increase in burial costs was blamed on a shortage of cemetery plots, while the hike in cremation costs was blamed on tighter environmental legislation which meant that equipment and premises needed to be updated.

The survey also drew attention to substantial regional variations in price. A burial in London's Southgate costs £6,140 compared to £1,797 in Manchester. The most expensive cremation price given was £3,200 by a funeral director in Luton, compared with the cheapest at £1,371 in Ipswich.

In Ireland, a funeral costs about €6,000 in Dublin and about €1,000 less outside the capital. More expensive burial plots and steeper labour costs account for the price difference. Currently, there is surprisingly little difference between the funeral costs of the wealthy and those of people of modest means. This is due to the fact that neither the funeral ritual nor funeral paraphernalia in Ireland have changed in decades. An Irish funeral tends to be more or less the same for a mendicant or a millionaire. The quality of a funeral is judged by the number of people in attendance, rather than by the amount of money expended on it. A large attendance is taken as a measure of the esteem in which the deceased was held, and this is something that cannot be bought.

The travelling community in Ireland tend to be an exception to the uniform, 'one size fits all', Irish funeral. Members of this minority group are fond of display. An Irishman who travels the final journey to the cemetery in a horse-drawn hearse and is buried in an expensive American steel casket, and over whom an elaborate marble memorial is erected, is likely to be a Traveller. However, the wealth generated by the Celtic Tiger may soon transform the simple Irish funeral into an occasion for conspicuous consumption. Should this happen, the United States – where a funeral can be as expensive as you want it to be – can offer an array of funeral merchandise to satisfy the most extravagant taste.

Take American coffins, for example, or 'caskets' as they are generally called. They are very impressive pieces of craftsmanship. The superb polished wood finish or the silk finish of a metal casket invites you to run your hand over it to feel its cool smoothness. In the upper price range, the lid clicks into place with such precision that neither air nor water can penetrate through to the interior. The sumptuous casket lining seems to guarantee an eternity of resting in peace. The most popular caskets are made from expensive materials such as hardwood, bronze, copper and steel of various gauges. They range in price from less than $1,000 dollars to more than $10,000. Popular models cost in the region of $4,000.

There is a bewildering choice of grave types in America, again with a wide variation in price. A single burial space could cost anything from $500 to $1,000, with a comparable fee charged for opening and closing the grave and associated paperwork. A concrete grave liner costs about $500, though you could pay in the region of $8,000 for a bronze 'vault' which fulfils the same function of protecting the casket after burial by taking the weight of the soil above it. A mausoleum allows for above ground burial. A purpose built structure, honeycombed with drawer-like slots, allows caskets to be slid into individual vaults. Because the building is fully enclosed and roofed, the caskets are protected from the elements. You will pay in the region of $4,000, for immurement in a mausoleum. An additional charge of about $400 covers the opening, closing and paperwork associated with this kind of vault burial.

Provision is made for companion burial, normally at about double the cost of a single burial. Graves may be excavated to a greater depth, 'double dug', allowing the first internment to be deeper in the ground and the second to be at the normal depth. In a mausoleum, a companion can be placed directly behind, below or beside the original occupant.

Cremation costs in the region of $300. Urns containing cremains may be buried, a process called 'inurnment', or placed in purpose built vaults and niches, at a fraction of the costs associated with body burial. At the same time, a niche for a family capable of taking up to four urns could cost $4,000.

Additional expenditure of a sum in the region of $400 is incurred with the purchase of a grave marker in a lawn cemetery or a name plate on a mausoleum or urn niche. An upright gravestone in a traditional cemetery is much more expensive.

How much does an American funeral cost? In the United States, funeral expenses are generally broken down into three main categories. Non-declinable charges are for funeral services which the customer must accept and pay for. They include the transportation of the remains to the funeral home, basic arrangements and supervision, and transfer of the remains to the cemetery or crematorium. Declinable charges are made for optional services such as preparation of the remains, visitation facilities, graveside attendance, merchandise items such as urns and acknowledgement cards. The third category, cash advanced items, are payments to third parties through the undertaker, such as crematorium charges, clergy honorariums, death certificates and many other necessary purchases and services. These outlays to third parties must be made by the funeral director on the day of the funeral and clients usually pay for them in advance.

Typically, for a fee of about $3,500, and upwards of an additional $1,000 for 'cash advanced items', a funeral home will provide the following fairly standard services: transportation of the remains to the funeral home; washing, embalming, dressing, casketing and facial make up of the remains; viewing or wake facilities for about four hours in any one day; service at a church; hearse to cemetery or crematorium, graveside attendance; stationery including 100 engraved acknowledgement cards, 100 printed prayer or service folders and a guest register book; obituary in the local newspaper. The casket and the burial or cremation are additional charges and can add very substantially to the final cost. A reasonable estimate, therefore, of the cost of an American funeral is $7,000 to $10,000, with the option, of course, of going much higher.

## *The Obituary*

Most people are likely to become the subject of an obituary. Though any published death notice may be described as such, it is not usual to apply the term to a simple announcement of a death and the funeral arrangements, such as is routinely submitted to newspapers by an undertaker and paid for by the family of the deceased. The term 'obituary' is reserved for a more lengthy account of the life of the deceased, commissioned by a newspaper or written by a staff member.

Obviously, the national press confines these little biographies to people who had occupied an important position in society. Local newspapers which include obituary columns extend the same treatment further down the social scale to local luminaries. However, journals of clubs and societies, parish newsletters and a myriad other little publications guarantee that few of us will go to our graves without the attentions of an amateur hagiographer.

The traditional posture of the obituary writer was to adopt a sombre tone and never to speak ill of the dead. Up to recently, these mournful enumerations of the CVs of the worthy dead did not provoke much interest among the newspaper-reading public. Nor did it provide much of a challenge for the writers of such columns. Indeed, obituary writing was often delegated to apprentice or incompetent journalists.

A revolution in the style and content of obituaries began in the mid-1980s when Hugh Massingberd was appointed obituaries editor at the *Daily Telegraph*, Britain's best selling daily broadsheet. His work raised the popularity of the *Telegraph's* obituary columns to the level of its sports pages. A further testament to the appeal of Massingberd's work was the publication of five volumes of his obituaries, all of which were eagerly devoured by a wide readership. The new dispensation spread to other British newspapers and also further afield, influencing

American and, to a lesser extent, Australian and Irish obituary styles as well. In time, the Massingberd approach may filter down to the humble parish newsletter. If it does, what kind of obituary can you expect? Basically, you can expect the truth: truth of the type that Oliver Cromwell demanded when he instructed Sir Peter Lely on how to paint his portrait: 'warts and all'.

First and foremost, the modern obituary writer seeks to turn out an entertaining piece of writing. Of almost equal importance is the desire to give the first historical assessment of the deceased person. Consequently, the solemn tone is gone, and the list of achievements has been augmented with quotations and anecdotes illustrating the foibles of the famous – the more bizarre the better. Strangely, obituary writers rarely take full advantage of the fact that the dead cannot sue for libel. They tend to use euphemism when recounting character defects, perhaps out of a sense of respect for the dead, or to save themselves from the accusation of taking cheap shots.

The modern obituary code is easily cracked. The seasoned reader will readily translate 'a convivial companion' as 'a drunk'; 'a tireless raconteur' as 'a relentless bore'. One who 'gave colorful accounts of his exploits' was a liar. An 'uncompromisingly direct ladies' man' was possibly a philandering rake. Even quite innocuous terms may have a hidden meaning: 'he never married' quite often is meant to convey that the deceased was gay.

The change in style has led to a consequent change in the criteria for selecting those considered worthy of an obituary in the national press. Obviously, anyone who is important will be given the treatment, but the old elite have been pushed aside in favour of people who were, in some way, interesting.

The change in the style of obituary writing has also provided an answer to the old conundrum, 'O death, where is thy sting?'

It is in the pen of the obituary writer!

# 7. After Death

In the thirteenth century a Chinese official named Sung T'su wrote a book on decomposition, It was intended to assist in the forensic examination of bodies when a death aroused suspicion. The book described in great detail the changes a body undergoes in the days, weeks and months after death. Remarkably, no significant studies of decomposition were undertaken for more than 750 years after Sun T'su's time. It was not until the 'body farm' was established in Knoxville, Tennessee by forensic anthropologist Dr Bill Bass in the 1980s that this important topic again became the subject of serious scientific research.

## The Body Farm

Dr Bass wanted to find out more about the processes and timetable of decomposition so that he could help law enforcement to estimate time since death more precisely. He went about his work in the most simple and direct manner. He secured the use of a couple of acres of woodland near the University of Tennessee and fenced it off from public access. He cleared an area in the centre and build a shed and some other basic facilities. Then he acquired unclaimed corpses from medical examiners. He brought the bodies to the 'farm' exposed them in different ways and, with the help of his students, studied carefully what happened. In his own words: 'we hid corpses in the woods. We locked them in the trunks and back seats of cars. We buried them in shallow graves. We submerged them in water. Then we studied and documented everything that happened to them, from the moment of death right up until the time, weeks or months later, when nothing remained but bone.'

The work of Dr Bass and his colleagues has proved invaluable to police forces round the world. In particular, it has helped to establish accurate 'time since death' estimates in murder cases involving victims whose bodies were not discovered until long after death. By establishing the sequence of arrival and departure of various species of insects, showing the significance of previously ignored items such as fly pupal cases, and quantifying the effect of temperature and moisture on decomposition, Dr Bass's team has given investigators a very useful weapon in the fight against serious crime.

Dr Bass and his body farm have a significance far beyond their forensic value. He has helped to bring decomposition out of the closet. Seven hundred and fifty years is a long time for science to have ignored a topic as important to the human race as our common destiny to die and decompose. Perhaps even scientists found it too distasteful to contemplate. Since the famous crime writer Patricia Cornwell visited the body farm in the 1990s and then featured it in one of her most popular works, which she called *The Body Farm* in salute to Dr Bass, the facility has been given a great deal of media attention. It has been the subject of several TV programmes and innumerable newspaper articles. Indeed, its existence has become part of our collective general knowledge. Dr Bass's own book about his life and work, *Death's Acre: Inside the legendary body farm*, also proved popular beyond expectations. Many people were so impressed with the work that they willed their bodies to be used for research purposes on the body farm. To date, over 300 bodies have been exposed on death's acre.

## Decomposition

The process of decomposition does not begin in the cemetery. Within minutes of death, nature's recycling machinery starts to operate. The ultimate end of the many processes that constitute decomposition, is the complete dismantling of the body. Left to nature, if the climate is sufficiently warm and humid and if insects have free access to it, a corpse may be reduced to a collection of bones in as little as two weeks. In less favourable conditions, the skeletonisation may take a year, and possibly much more. Further, more protracted measures erode the bones and finally reduce them to dust. Bone destruction takes time and may not be completed for centuries.

Decomposition is best understood as a transition process which, when complete, returns the body to the elements from which it was originally created. The combined action of autolysis (self-digestion), putrefaction (the action of bacteria, fungi and protozoa) and diagenesis (the degrading of bone) result in complex structures composed of proteins, carbohydrates, sugars, collagen and lipids returning to their simplest building blocks.

Modern, forensically inspired studies of decomposition have yielded vast amounts of new information, helping us to understand what precisely is going on at each stage of destruction. Traditionally, decomposition was regarded as a progression from dead to dust in four stages. The phases were named: fresh, bloat, decay, and dry.

## FRESH

The first, 'fresh' stage of decomposition is characterised by the body's own intrinsic resources turning against itself. In life, digestive enzymes in the gastro-intestinal tract break down the complex carbohydrate and protein molecules in food into simpler molecules, which can be absorbed into the blood stream to nourish and energise the body. The living body protects itself against these caustic chemicals by lining the walls of the stomach, and digestive system in general, with a coating of mucous. Anyone who has experienced heartburn will be aware of how corrosive these digestive juices can be. The absence of mucous protection after death results in the eventual perforation of the gastro-intestinal tract and the seepage of digestive fluids, including hydrochloric acid, into the abdomen and chest cavity. In this way, the body starts to literally digest itself.

A similar, microcosmic breakdown begins throughout the body. Cells deprived of oxygen and poisoned by carbon dioxide and other waste products start to self destruct. Enzymes working from inside the cell walls start to dissolve and to rupture the cells, to break the connections between cells and to release nutrient rich fluids. This process starts in the brain cells a few minutes after death and progresses most rapidly in organs with a high water content. Organs rich in enzymes, like the pancreas and liver are also quick to digest themselves.

Initially, the ravages of the 'fresh' stage show no visible outer signs, as most of the damage is internal. After a few days, fluid filled blisters begin to appear, the skin loosens and may become detached from the body in large sheets.

## BLOAT

The second, 'bloat', stage is driven by microorganisms. The work of bacteria and other simple forms of life begins to transform the complex molecules of the human body into simple molecules, liquids and gases. Putrefaction is a more accurate technical term for this process. The formation of hydrogen sulphide (the rotten egg gas), methane, ammonia, carbon dioxide, hydrogen and other gases swell the body. These gases are first generated within the digestive tract as this is the centre of a spreading putrefaction. Gases trapped in this area cause distension of the abdomen. Victims of drowning often bob back to the surface at this stage of decomposition due to additional buoyancy, but the body may easily release abdominal gases through the mouth and anus and sink again after a short time.

As the process accelerates, microorganisms attacking the defenceless body increase rapidly both in number and type. According to Dr Arpad Vass, an expert on decomposition, 'with the exception of microorganisms living in deep sea vents, every microorganism known is involved in some aspect of the human decomposition cycle from Acetobacter to Zooglea...literally hundreds of species are involved in the decompositional process and decomposition would not progress without them.' Equally impressive is the number of substances produced in the breakdown of the human body. Dr Vass is quoted as saying that there is a hodgepodge of about 450 known chemicals released in the decomposition process.

As putrefaction radiates out from the abdomen to the extremities, gas production commences in all areas: organs, muscles, blood vessels. Trapped gases, with names of memorable foulness such as 'cadaverine' and 'putrescine,' swell the whole body. Limbs, trunk and face inflate; abdominal organs protrude through the vaginal and rectal openings; the eyes bulge and the tongue protrudes. The drowned resurface again at this stage of decomposition. This 'second flotation' is characterised by a much more stable buoyancy due to the additional quantities of gases, the even spread through the body and the lack of escape routes.

Indeed the build up of gases may be powerful enough to inflate the abdomen to bursting point. In 2004, the *Houston*

*Chronicle* reported that the decomposing remains of a 60-ton sperm whale exploded on a busy Taiwan street, showering near-by cars and shops with blood and organs and stopping traffic for hours. The 56-foot long dead whale had been on a truck head-ed for an autopsy at a university when gases from internal decay caused its entrails to explode. Human detonation is not unknown.

The pressure of pent up gases forces fluids out of the cells and blood vessels and into the body cavity. Fluids from the lungs ooze out of the mouth and nose. Bacterial action blisters the skin and turns it blue and green in colour.

DECAY

The bloated body eventually collapses. A large volume of fluid seeps out and drains into the surrounding area. The exposed parts of the corpse are now black and there is a very strong stench of decay. Microbe activity continues, joined by insects if they can gain access, and between them they eventually con-sume all of the flesh. As the body enters the 'dry' stage of decomposition, the absence of soft food makes it unattractive to most insects, apart from beetles. With their chewing mouth parts they are better adapted to the consumption of skin and lig-aments.

DRY

The dry body decays very slowly. It takes 40-50 years for bones to become dry and brittle in a coffin. While both acid and peaty soil gradually dissolve bones, they may last for hundreds of years in soil of neutral acidity. Exposed bones begin to bleach within the first year. Calcium potassium and magnesium leach out and algae and moss begin to grow on them. Within ten years further deterioration is seen as the outer layer erodes away and large cracks appear.

## INSECTS

Whereas embalming slows down the process of decomposition, sometimes very considerably, the presence of insects accelerates it. Normally, a dead body is stored in a manner that protects it from the depredations of carnivorous insects, but in times of war and great natural disaster, bodies may remain out in the open and unattended. The bodies of murder victims, the elderly dying alone, and people who suffer accidents in remote areas may not be discovered for quite a while after death. Bodies in such circumstances may be subjected to every weapon in nature's recycling arsenal. Where decomposition is concerned, flies are nature's weapons of mass destruction.

Flies are attracted to bodies from the moment of death and are capable of detecting a corpse very quickly. On a warm summer's day, blowflies, bluebottles and house flies in their thousands will swarm all over a body, soaking up exuded fluids in their spongy mouths and laying eggs in dark, damp bodily orifices, such as the mouth, nostrils, ears and eyes. A female fly can lay hundreds of eggs at a time. The yellow-white masses of fly eggs hatch into maggots in four to six hours. Prime sites near moist openings give the maggots the best start in life. Like the adult flies, the maggots feed off the fluids first, but later they enter the body through the natural openings or wounds and spread throughout as the tissues decay.

The great number of maggots and the speed with which they populate a body was strikingly demonstrated to a group of trainee investigators when they slid the remains of a murder victim into a body bag, placed it in a van and drove it back to an investigation facility. Only a handful of maggots was visible at the collection point, but when the body was removed from the bag at the end of the journey, a swarm of tens of thousands were crawling all over it. Part of the explanation given to the students by the experienced officer was that maggots do not like the sunshine and burrow beneath the skin until darkness. They had resurfaced during the body bag trip.

Maggots move through the body as a mass, sharing digestive secretions, tearing dead tissue with special mouth hooks and spreading bacteria. These diminutive carnivores, if present in sufficient numbers, can consume up to 40 pounds of human flesh in a 24 hour period. Consequently, they increase greatly in size in a matter of days and pass rapidly through several developmental stages.

When a maggot reaches a certain stage of maturity, it moves away from the body, finds a suitable pupation site, usually in nearby soil, and encases itself in a hard shell. After about ten days, it emerges from its cocoon as a mature fly. It mates, returns to the corpse to feed on protein and then lays a new generation of maggot eggs on the corpse

As the rate of decay increases, more gases and fluids are released attracting other species of insect. Many of the new arrivals are predators with as much interest in the eggs, maggots and flies on and round the corpse as the corpse itself. The dead body becomes a venue where insects act out a Darwinian struggle for the survival of the fittest. Wasps attack flies on the wing. Parasitoid wasps lay their eggs inside maggots so their emerging larvae may eat their way out of a living supply of protein. Beetles dine on maggots. Late arriving species of fly compensate for their tardiness by giving birth to fully formed maggots rather than laying eggs.

As the body reaches the 'dry' stage, one species of insect after another loses interest in it. Various types of moth, including the ones that consume our clothes, are among the last forms of life to leave a human carcass. They consume human hair and lay their eggs where their larvae can feed on it. When the last moth deserts the body and blunders off into the night, only the bones remain, and perhaps some bits of skin and flesh that have dried out and become too hard for consumption.

In circumstances in which a body is unprotected, the presence of larger carnivores, such as rodents or dogs, results in its disposal much more quickly. The other crucial environmental factors are temperature and moisture. The presence of both speed up the decomposition. However, in arctic and desert environments a body dries out very rapidly and consequently may be preserved indefinitely. Bodies that are buried, or submerged in water have different rates of decomposition.

## The Maggot's Message

Of the life forms that facilitate the process of decomposition, maggots are generally regarded as the most repulsive. Magnification under an electron microscope does little to alter this impression as the creatures look fearsome up close. However, it is worth remembering that in recent years the reputation of the maggot has been transformed. Specially bred maggots are now used quite extensively in mainstream medicine in the treatment of infected wounds. The maggots, at an early stage of development, are placed in an infected wound, held in

FIGURE 8: THE MICRO-SURGEON MAGNIFIED: THE MAGGOT IS ARMED WITH TUSK-LIKE PROJECTIONS — MOUTH HOOKS — WHICH CAN SHRED DECAYED FLESH AND DIRECT IT INTO ITS DIGESTIVE TRACT. THESE USEFUL INSECTS ARE WIDELY EMPLOYED IN MEDICINE AS MICRO-SURGEONS.
(ELECTRON MICROGRAPH: S. LINDSAY)

place by bandages and allowed to consume the dead and damaged tissue over a few days. It has been observed that the maggots will not damage live tissue and will entirely clean up wounds that have been the despair of doctors, in a matter of a few days. Apparently, in many cultures, maggots have been used for this purpose for hundreds of years.

The fact that maggots will not damage living tissue conveys a very clear message: a corpse is not a human being. Decomposition, and the other unpleasant procedures such as autopsies, embalming, cremation and burial, are easier to come to terms with if we regard a dead body in the same way as we would regard nail parings, hair trimmings or amputated limbs. Certainly, a corpse should be treated with dignity and respect but not reverence. A body is often referred to as 'the remains' and that is an accurate description. The life, the animus, the soul, the essence is gone.

# 8. Afterlife

The idea of an afterlife is firmly embedded in all the major religions. Up to recent times, only a tiny minority of people rejected such a belief. It seemed self evident that on the point of death, some essential element, usually referred to as the soul, left the body. Even the vocabulary of death conveyed this notion. The dead were referred to as 'the departed'; they were said to have 'gone' or 'passed away'. Further proof of an afterlife was available in sacred scripture. Both the *Bible* and the *Koran* contained many passages which referred to an existence after death in heaven or hell. The writings of theologians provided additional details on the nature of both destinations.

In the modern secular world, it is quite common to believe that death involves complete annihilation, thus downgrading what used to be regarded as 'the immortal soul' to a mere sense of self, which perishes with the body. Consciousness, many believe, has no independent existence outside of the body; it cannot continue after death because the body is its life support system.

Clearly, only one of these points of view can be correct. While most of the evidence to support the idea of an afterlife comes from sacred writings, the authority of which is rejected by non-believers, in recent years new evidence has been discovered which has caused many people to reflect further on the matter. Before examining the new data, this chapter reviews the life after death teachings of some of the major religions.

## *Christianity and the Afterlife*

Christian theologians developed a very detailed concept of the afterlife over two millennia. What happens after death was, for centuries, a subject of great interest and intense debate among church thinkers. Schools of thought found acceptance for a while, only to be superseded by other, more seductive notions. The popes and the councils of the church adjudicated in controversies, condemning some ideas and approving others. By the time of the Reformation, the main ideas regarding the afterlife had been fairly well established. However, when Christian unity came to an end in the sixteenth century, the nature of the afterlife again became a major area of disagreement. The newly established churches were free to reject large chunks of Roman Catholic dogma and to develop their own ideas. Currently, there are over 1,000 different Christian denominations in the USA alone and an estimated 2,000 worldwide. Since teachings on the afterlife have continued to develop right up to the present day, it is difficult to be definitive on what exactly Christians now believe in that regard. While the following paragraphs are based on traditional Christian teaching, the views of major Christian denominations are referred to where significant differences exist.

DAY OF JUDGEMENT
The Roman Catholic Church teaches that judgement of an individual's merit, and consequently the kind of afterlife to which he is consigned, takes place immediately after death. A person who dies in mortal sin is immediately sent to the fires of hell. Souls that are perfectly pure are at once admitted to heaven.

Those who leave their bodies while still in need of spiritual purification are sent to purgatory to be cleansed. This immediate processing of the soul is called the 'particular judgement'. Souls are said to be internally illuminated as to their own innocence or guilt and to automatically proceed to heaven, hell or purgatory.

Some Christians have disputed this version of events. They hold that the soul is temporarily destroyed, and subsequently revived on the final day of judgement. Others believe that it remains in a state of suspended animation or 'soul slumber' until the end of the world. John Calvin taught that the final destiny of the soul was not determined until the last day.

All Christians believe that on the last day, Christ will come to judge the living and the dead. On the day of judgement, a trumpet will awaken the dead and everyone of them will arise. Every soul will return to the body it vacated after death. Christ will then appear in the heavens, seated on a cloud and surrounded by his armies of angels. The angels will bring the living and the risen dead before him for judgement. Through a divine illumination, everyone will become fully aware of his own moral condition and that of everyone else. Every act, good and evil, will be made known to everyone: sins forgiven and unforgiven, every idle word, every secret thought. The just will not be embarrassed by the public exposure of their faults

The resurrected bodies will be immortal. This will be a source of great joy to the saved, but not to the damned. For them, the reunited and immortal body will be no more than another channel through which to endure pain. The wicked, according to the *Apocalypse*, 'shall seek death and shall not find it, shall desire to die, and death shall fly from them'.

HEAVEN
In the *Bible*, heaven is variously called: the kingdom of heaven, the kingdom of God, the heavenly Jerusalem, paradise, the great

reward, and the eternal inheritance. It is described as the dwelling place of God and the angels and the abode of the souls of the just. It is a place of perfect happiness in which the blessed live for all eternity, and every wish finds adequate satisfaction. However, since the blessed no longer have the power of choosing to do evil, all their wishes are of the most wholesome kind. The chief joy of the souls in heaven is being able to perceive God directly. The ability of the blessed to see God, that is enjoy the 'beatific vision', is one of the fundamental beliefs of Christian Churches.

There are many other lesser joys in heaven. There is no more sorrow of any kind. The will of the blessed is in complete harmony with the will of God. Whereas the blessed may feel displeasure at the sins of the living, they experience no real pain. They enjoy the company of Christ and of the angels and the saints. They have the pleasure of meeting again with those who were dear to them on earth.

After the resurrection, they will be able to enjoy reunion with their now 'glorified' body, which, though in many respects it will be the same as the body they occupied when they were alive as ordinary human beings, it will be more subtle and more powerful. The glorified bodies of all saved souls will possess four qualities that they did not have on earth. First of all, they will be incapable of feeling pain. Secondly, they will shine brightly with different degrees of radiance: some like the sun, some like the moon, some like the stars. Thirdly, they will have agility of movement, being capable of moving with the utmost speed with the greatest of ease. Fourthly, the body will become totally subject to the desires of the spirit, becoming spirit like itself.

There are various degrees of ecstasy in heaven, corresponding to the various degrees of merit. Theologians base this belief on Christ's statement in Matthew's gospel that those who hear the word of God bear fruit: 'in one case a hundredfold, in another sixty, and in another thirty'. The measure of exaltation is reflected both in the intensity of the beatific vision and the level of the lesser pleasures. Certain categories of the blessed are singled out for special recognition. Martyrs, virgins and doctors of the church, in particular, wear special crowns of gold in recognition of victories won in times of trial.

## HELL

Theologians have distinguished four different hells. The first is a place of eternal punishment for the damned. The second, purgatory, is a place of temporary detention where souls ultimately bound for heaven are cleansed by suffering. The third and fourth are known as limbo. Limbo of the infants is for those who die without baptism, that is with the stain of original sin on their souls, but without any other sins: essentially infants who died at birth or shortly afterwards. The limbo of the fathers was a place of rest for those who died before the time of Christ but against whom heaven was temporarily closed due to the sin of Adam.

The existence of hell as a place for those who died in mortal sin, where they will be punished for all eternity, is one of strongest and most longstanding beliefs of all the Christian churches. The view that the punishment of the damned is not eternal but that after a certain amount of time they will either be annihilated or taken into heaven, is considered to be heretical. St Matthew's gospel is very specific in this regard: 'Then he [Christ] will say to those at his left hand, "Depart from me you cursed, into the eternal fire prepared for the devil and his angels..." and they will go away into eternal punishment.' Many other biblical passages refer to an eternal and unquenchable fire. No Christian church ever prays for the damned in hell as their condition is deemed to be justly deserved and unchangeable.

The greatest pain in hell is the consciousness of being irrevocably excluded from the presence of God. The damned are humiliated and depressed by recollecting that, for temporary pleasures, they have forfeited the greatest reward imaginable. In addition, the damned are tortured by real fire which continually burns without the necessity of renewed fuel and causes pain without destroying the soul. The damned never experience the least pleasure. The company of the damned is vile to one another, and they engage in outbursts of hatred, blame and gloating over the suffering of their companions. Their reunification with the body after the resurrection only causes an increase in their pains. The pains of hell differ in intensity according to the level of evil, the more evil having a greater capacity for suffering which is accommodated to the utmost.

## PURGATORY

All those who die with minor sins on their souls go to purgatory immediately after death. Purgatory is like a medieval prison. It is a grim place of incarceration and severe punishment, but the inmates are released after a period. The length of the sentence depends on the amount of suffering still owed for sins committed on earth. Though sins may have been forgiven, a sinner is not completely absolved until the appropriate level of retribution has been exacted. Once sinners have been purified, they are admitted to heaven.

The concept of purgatory was clearly defined by the Council of Trent and relies for its authority on decisions of church councils rather than any clear passage from the Bible. Luther, Calvin and other protestant reformers rejected the doctrine of purgatory, and the Roman Catholic Church alone subscribes to its existence.

The nature of the suffering in purgatory is similar to that in hell and includes both the pain of separation from God and the pain of fire. Some of the great Christian authorities, including St Augustine, Gregory the Great and St Thomas Aquinas refer to the pains of purgatory as being more severe than any pain experienced in life. Some thinkers suggested that uncertainty is another one of the punishments of purgatory. By this they mean that the inmates do not know whether they are in purgatory, from which they will eventually be released, or in hell where they will remain. This concept was rejected because the doctrine of the particular judgement states that a sinner becomes aware of his level of guilt and destination immediately after death.

Like the damned in hell, the souls in purgatory can do nothing to help themselves, but the living can aid them. It is possible for the living to reduce the pains of those suffering in purgatory by praying for them, having masses said for them and by obtaining indulgences on their behalf. An indulgence cuts down a sinner's purgatorial sentence by various amounts. A plenary indulgence wipes out the sentence in full. An indulgence usually involves praying, doing good works, giving money to the poor and contributing to worthy causes such as church building funds. Plenary indulgences are proclaimed by the pope, lesser indulgences can be proclaimed by cardinals and bishops from time to time. Such proclamations detail all the conditions that need to be fulfilled for a sinner in purgatory to benefit from the indulgence.

A controversy over indulgences was the occasion for Martin Luther's break with Rome in 1517. At that time the pope had declared a plenary indulgence for anybody who contributed to the building of the new St Peter's Basilica in Rome, while fulfilling a number of other conditions as well. His agent in Germany, John Tetzel, is reputed to have preached that as soon as the money hit the bottom of the chest, the soul popped out of purgatory. This was a travesty of the doctrine of indulgences, but apparently Tetzel was more of a salesman than a theologian. To this day, reformed churches are scathing about indulgences.

Many people find that the teachings on purgatory are hard to reconcile with a modern sense of justice and fair play. A sinner in purgatory who has friends still on earth who are willing to assist him with prayers, indulgences and masses, is released more quickly than the poor abandoned souls. This is analogous to having a smart lawyer to get you out of prison.

LIMBO

Between the fall of Adam and Eve and the resurrection of Christ, no soul could go to heaven. The souls of those who had merited heaven were accommodated for the time being in

FIGURE 9: 'HE DESCENDED INTO HELL': MANY CHRISTIANS BELIEVE THAT THIS SENTENCE FROM THE APOSTLE'S CREED MEANS THAT, AFTER HIS CRUCIFIXION, CHRIST WENT TO THE PART OF HELL IN WHICH THE RIGHTEOUS DEAD WERE CONFINED AND BROUGHT THEM TO HEAVEN. *THE RISEN CHRIST RESCUES THE DEAD* BY PETER VON CORNELIUS (1783-1867) GRAPHICALLY ILLUSTRATES THIS INTERPRETATION.

limbo, described by theologians as a state or place of happiness. After his death on the cross and before he rose from the dead three days later, Jesus Christ went to limbo to inform the souls there that their salvation was at hand. This is what is meant by the line in the apostles creed which states: 'He descended into hell'. Shortly after that, limbo of the fathers ceased to exist.

Limbo of the infants seems to have been willed into existence to solve a tricky theological problem. Christians believe that humans are born into this world in a state of original sin which can be wiped out by baptism alone. Therefore, unbaptised infants who die, die in sin and are consequently excluded from heaven. No scriptural passage gives a clear account of what is the eternal destiny of these unfortunate babies, so it was up to theologians to come up with an answer. St Augustine believed that such children went to hell for all eternity and suffered a mild version of the torture of the damned. He was prepared to go so far as to accept that their condition was probably such that it was preferable to non-existence. This teaching persisted for several hundred years until it was decided that the infants were not subjected to hell fire but only excluded for ever from the beatific vision. But since this is regarded as the most severe punishment in hell, the supposed lot of the infants was not improved very much. Thomas Aquinas came up with a more acceptable doctrine. He said that though the infants are excluded from the beatific vision, their total acceptance of the will of God allows them to be perfectly happy, even though they are aware of what they have lost through no fault of their. Later he decided on a simpler solution: that the infants have no knowledge of the supernatural destiny they have missed out on, and therefore are not pained by it. St Thomas's doctrine was further developed so that by the beginning of the twentieth century the great majority of Roman Catholic theologians maintained that the children's limbo is a state of perfect natural happiness.

It is difficult to find out what the current teachings are on limbo as it is omitted from the latest version of the Catholic Catechism. It would appear that limbo itself is now in limbo.

It may not remain there for very long, however. In 1984 the German theologian Cardinal Joseph Ratzinger, the head of the Congregation for the Doctrine of the Faith, stated his personal view of Limbo as follows: 'Limbo has never been a defined truth of faith. Personally, speaking as a theologian and not as head of the Congregation, I would drop something that has always been only a theological hypothesis'. Cardinal Ratzinger was elected as Pope Benedict XVI in 2005.

# Other Heavens and Other Hells

Christianity, with worldwide membership of its various sects topping 2.1 billion, has more adherents than any other religion. The adherents of Islam, the Muslims, are second to Christians in numerical strength, with an estimated membership of over 1.3 billion. Islamic teachings on the afterlife have much in common with those of Christianity, with belief in the day of judgement, heaven, hell and eternal damnation. However, some of the details differ, especially Muslim heaven, which is described in sensual detail in the *Koran* and other Islamic writings.

ISLAM
One of the cartoons that outraged the Islamic world in early 2006 depicted Mohammad up in the clouds addressing a queue of newly-arrived suicide bombers/martyrs with the words: 'Stop, stop, we ran out of virgins!' The caption refers to the popular view of Islamic heaven as a place of luxury and heavenly sex, starkly contrasting with the chaste and Spartan Paradise of the Christians. To what extent is this based on Islamic scripture?

Two texts form the basis of Islam. The *Koran* is the more sacred. Muslims believe it to be the literal word of God as revealed to Muhammad. The less authoritative *Hadith* or Islamic tradition, is a record of the deeds and sayings of the prophet, his family and companions.

The Koran states that in paradise there are rivers of water, rivers of milk, rivers of wine and rivers of honey, and that the people there wear silken garments and recline on raised thrones. Bunches of fruit hang close within their reach. Silver cups and crystal glasses are passed round amongst them. Boys of perpetual youth are there to serve them with wine.

Like Christian heaven, Muslim paradise has its gradations. According to the *Koran* 'Those foremost in obedience to Allah will be nearest to Allah in the gardens of delight. They shall recline on jewelled couches face to face, and there shall wait on them immortal youths with bowls and ewers and a cup of purest wine (that will neither pain their heads nor take away their reason); with fruits of their own choice and flesh of fowls that they relish. And theirs shall be the dark-eyed houris (virgins), chaste as hidden pearls: a reward for their deeds…created for them houris of equal age, loving their husbands only…'

Paradise is described in the *Hadith* in the same sensual manner: the inhabitants dwell in massive palaces: 'the smallest reward for the people of Paradise is an abode where there are 80,000 servants and 72 wives, over which stands a dome decorated with pearls, aquamarine, and ruby'.

Until the Day of Judgment, deceased souls remain in their graves waiting for the resurrection, but they begin to feel immediately a sense of their destiny to come. Those bound for hell will suffer in their graves, while those bound for heaven will be in peace until that time.

On the last day, everybody will be judged by Allah. The resurrected then pass over hell on a narrow bridge in order to enter paradise. Those who fall, weighted by their bad deeds, will remain in hell. The level depends on the degree of culpability. Suffering is both physical and spiritual.

It is not clear whether hell is for all eternity or whether, like purgatory, sinners are allowed into paradise after a period of purification. Some commentators believe the latter to be the case for Muslims but that non-Muslim will be punished eternally. Other Muslim commentators, noting that Allah can rescue people from hell as he chooses, and that he is merciful and compassionate, have suggested that eventually hell will be empty.

JEWISH AFTERLIFE

The Jews believe in an afterlife but put far less emphasis on it than other religions. Most of their focus is on this life. The Jewish concept of an afterlife has changed and developed over the centuries. At an early stage, afterlife for the Jews consisted of a shadowy existence much less satisfactory than real life; something like the Hades of the ancient world. Other ideas were imported from other philosophies. Because they have no dogmatic teachings on the afterlife, Jews can believe that the dead go to a place like the Christian heaven, or that souls are reincarnated and go through several different lives, or that the dead remain in their graves until resurrected by the Messiah. Similarly, they may believe in a traditional hell or the annihilation of the souls of the wicked.

# Evidence: The Well to Hell

Many believe that heaven and hell are not just spiritual states of being, but real physical locations. The *Bible* places heaven somewhere in the firmament among the stars, but its exact position was never pinpointed. However, it was generally accepted that hell was situated somewhere beneath the ground. The *Bible* seems to indicate that hell is within the earth, for it describes it as an abyss to which the wicked descend. The *Bible* also refers to the earth opening up and the wicked sinking down to hell. This view was accepted by most Christian Churches up as far as the twentieth century and many fundamentalist Christians still believe that the damned are undergoing the most horrendous torture, literally beneath our feet. Mount Hekla, an active volcano in Iceland, was regarded as one of hell's gates, and it was reported in medieval times that the screams of the damned could be heard by people passing close to it.

There is no reason to believe that modern technology has ever been used to probe outer space for evidence of heaven, or to burrow underground in search of hell. However, a story has been circulating for about fifteen years, alleging that a team of scientists accidentally came within nine miles of hell. The story was broadcast on several American TV channels: Trinity Broadcasting in 1989, Praise the Lord in February 1990, and on Midnight Cry the following month. It has had exposure in the print media and can be found on very many internet sites.

The origin of the story was said to be a respected Finnish newspaper called *Ammennusastia*. It told of a group of geological explorers attempting to dig a deep well in Siberia. After the drill bit had gone about nine miles into the earth's crust, it suddenly started to spin out of control. The scientists concluded that it must have reached a hollow pocket in the earth's crust. They were surprised to discover that the temperature readings at that level had gone up to over one thousand degrees Celsius, much higher than expected. The scientists had special supersensitive microphones which they used to listen to the movements of the earth at various depths. When they lowered a microphone into the void, they were surprised to hear high pitched sounds. They suspected that the noises were generated by their own equipment, but when the microphone was properly adjusted they discovered that the noise was, in fact, a human voice screaming in pain. Beyond that voice, they heard several thousand, perhaps millions, of other voices also shrieking out in agony. Half the scientists immediately quit because of fear. Dr Azzacov is quoted as saying: 'As a communist I don't believe in heaven or the *Bible* but as a scientist I now believe in hell'.

The story was seized upon by fundamentalist Christian groups as proof of the existence of hell. Among the corroborative evidence currently offered on various websites, are scans of newspaper cuttings of the original article, and a downloadable recording of the screams of the damned, which the scientists allegedly taped before their microphone melted.

However, the story fails to stand up to close scrutiny. *Ammennusastia* is the monthly magazine of a Finnish Christian group, not a respected Finnish newspaper. That journal picked up the story from the letters page of a daily paper. The letter writer got it from a Christian newsletter, *Vaeltajat*, published by a Finnish group of missionaries. The editor of *Vaeltajat* said his source was a Norwegian teacher who had heard it on a TV broadcast in the United States. Clearly, believers in the US thought that the original source of the story was a Finnish journalist, while the Finns believed a US broadcaster was the source. Like many urban legends, the story goes round in circles. If the well to hell story proves anything it is that, as far as belief in matters metaphysical is concerned, our own personal experience is now more influential than the say-so of ancient texts. Let's leave the last word on the topic to a US evangelist: 'Folks...if this is a trick of the Devil, he sure has blown it, because I know of about 2,000 people that have found Christ because of it'.

# Evidence: Near Death Experiences

Dr Raymond Moody, an American academic, wrote a book in 1975 entitled *Life After Life*. It documents the experiences of people who had been technically dead for short periods and who claimed to have had dramatic experiences during their time out. All of the experiences were remarkably similar. They involved some or all of the following features: the impression of being outside of the body, sometimes floating above it and being able to view themselves and others from that perspective; an awareness of moving through a dark tunnel towards a bright light which often turned into a powerful being; meeting with departed relatives and friends; having feelings of great comfort and security; a strong desire to remain and not to return to the body. The experience, in most cases, was life altering. Fear of death was no longer a factor in their lives afterwards, and there was a tendency to become more spiritual and less materialistic.

Most of the stories were related by people whom Dr Moody was able to interview, but he claims that people right through history have reported similar experiences. There are scattered references to comparable episodes in medical literature as far back as the nineteenth century, and the writings of Gregory of Tours and the Venerable Bede in the Dark Ages relate similar stories. The testimony of a soldier in Plato's *Republic* assure us that the experience was known in antiquity.

Because this phenomenon had not been previously named, Dr Moody coined the phrase 'near-death experience' to cover it. The term is now normally abbreviated to the initial letters 'NDE' which are always capitalised. Had Dr Moody realised that NDEs would become such a major area of research and controversy, perhaps he would have made an effort to devise a better acronym.

It might seem strange that something as remarkable as NDE had to wait until the twentieth century to be named. The explanation is simple: advances in cardiopulmonary resuscitation (CPR) have increased the number of people who have been revived some time after the cessation of all clinical signs of life. Today, a significant portion of resuscitated patients, in some studies a reported 60 percent or more, claim to have had an NDE. Before the mid-twentieth century, what is now routine practice in hospital emergency rooms, would have been regarded as a miracle. At that time, those whose hearts and lungs stopped functioning for the shortest period of time, remained dead in all but the most exceptional cases.

The calibre of the researchers and the quality of the work produced by many people involved in the study of NDEs requires that their findings be taken seriously. Dr Moody himself holds two doctorates, one in philosophy and one in psychology. He also has a medical degree from the Medical College of Georgia. Dr Kenneth Ring who followed up on Dr Moody's work is Professor of Psychology at the University of Connecticut.

Dr Ring managed to contact and question over 100 people who experienced the near-death phenomena. On the basis of his researches, he was able to draw a number of interesting conclusions. No one type of person is more likely than another to have an NDE; it cuts across race, gender, age, education, marital status and social class. Medication, drugs and anaesthesia do not appear to have a role in producing the characteristics of a NDE. Previous religious orientation has no bearing on the experience. An atheist is as likely to have an NDE as a religious person. After a near-death experience, many people reported a loss of fear of death and a greater appreciation of life

Other researchers have shown that the cultural differences between NDEs is remarkably narrow. The stories related by Europeans and Americans do not differ from those experienced by people in India, Japan and China, remarkably different cultures.

The most interesting and most closely studied aspect of the NDE is the out of body experience (OBE). When a patient feels that he has left his body, he will typically feel himself hovering above the doctors who are attending him. Afterwards, he may be able to relate details of what went on in the emergency room, or other parts of the hospital, while he was clinically dead. Some of these stories are quite remarkable and baffle explanation.

## THE LANCET

In December 2001 the authoritative British medical journal, *The Lancet*, published the results of an extensive scientific investigation into near-death experiences. It focused on 344 heart patients in Holland. All had been resuscitated in coronary units in ten selected hospitals. The purpose of the study was to discover the frequency and causes of the experience. The investigation included follow-up questioning of patients after a two year and an eight year interval with a view to establishing the long term impact of an NDE. The study is unusual in that all resuscitated patients in each hospital over a period were included in the study. In most other NDE studies there is a large element of self-selection; that is, people come forward in response to requests by researchers.

All of the patients had been clinically dead, that is, unconscious for some minutes due to lack of blood supply to the brain. This fact was established mainly by electrocardiogram records. Had CPR not been performed within five or ten minutes in these circumstances, irreparable brain damage and death would have followed.

A few days after resuscitation, patients were asked whether they could recall the period of unconsciousness and, if so, what exactly they could recall about it. Their responses were recorded and analysed. Various other details, personal and medical were also recorded regarding each patient, including race, sex, religion and standard of education; whether they had previously heard of NDE; type and dosage of drugs before, during and after resuscitation.

Eighteen percent of patients, 62 out of the 344, had some recollection of the period of clinical death. Of those, one third had a superficial NDE and two thirds had what the researchers called a 'core' near-death experience. For each of the 62 patients, the episode included some or all of the following: awareness of being dead, positive emotions, out of body experience, moving through a tunnel, communication with light, observation of colours, observation of celestial landscape, meeting with deceased persons, life review.

After two years, a follow up of patients who had had an NDE and a control group of patients who experienced nothing while clinically dead, indicated significant differences in outlook based on their answers to a series of life-change questions. Those who had the experience showed an increase in belief in an afterlife and a decrease in fear of death compared with people who had not had the experience. The people who had deeper, more intense NDEs scored much higher in spiritual items such as an interest in the meaning of life.

The eight year follow up showed that those who did not have an NDE still, generally, did not believe in an afterlife, while belief in an afterlife and lack of fear of death among those who had experienced an NDE was stronger than ever. The study also found that all the patients who had had an NDE could recall the details of the experience almost exactly, even after the passage of eight years.

The study concluded that physiological, psychological and medical factors, including medication, could not account for the occurrence of NDE. The researchers also commented that: 'the long lasting transformational effects of an experience that lasts for only a few minutes of cardiac arrest is a surprising and unexpected finding.' The report also pointed out that though similar experiences can be induced by electrical stimulation of the brain and by the administration of drugs, the induced experiences do not result in life transforming processes. Looking to the future, the report recommended that NDE research should be concentrated on specific elements, such as out of body experiences.

## OUT OF BODY EXPERIENCES

The authors of *The Lancet* study recorded one fascinating out of body experience. A comatose patient was brought into one of the participating hospitals. The 44 year old man had been found in a state of unconsciousness in a meadow by passers by. He had turned blue due to oxygen deprivation. It proved so difficult to revive him that the CPR team considered giving up. At one point it was necessary to insert a tube into the man's throat and in the process a nurse removed his false teeth. She stored them in the drawer of a 'crash car', a trolley used for transporting medicines to and from wards. After about an hour and a half the vital signs were sufficiently strong to remove the patient to the intensive care ward, still in a deep coma. A week later, the nurse was passing through the ward when she was hailed by the patient. She had never before spoken to him. He asked her to return his dentures, telling her where she had put them. On further questioning, the patient said that on the night he had been brought to the hospital emergency room, he was able to observe, from a perspective above the bed, both himself and the CPR team which was working on him. He described the small emergency room in detail, the members of the medical team and the conversation that was going on between them.

An out of body experience like that described above, in which a patient acquires information which could not be gained through normal sensory perception, is called a *veridical* OBE. Many such OBEs have been recorded and they seem to defy explanation.

A frequently quoted veridical OBE concerns a heart patient known as 'Maria'. Having suffered a heart attack while visiting Seattle, she was taken at night to the coronary care unit of Harborview Medical Center. Three days after admission she suffered cardiac arrest. She was resuscitated quickly and her condition stabilised. Later the same day she gave a detailed account to a social worker who had been assigned to her of an out of body experience. She claimed that she found herself looking down from the ceiling at the doctors and nurses who were working on her body. She was able to describe both the staff and the fittings in the emergency room. She described finding herself outside the building as if she had just 'thought herself' there. She gave an accurate account of the area around the entrance, including the fact that it was reached by a curved one-way road. She then noticed an object on the ledge of a third storey window. She discovered that it was a shoe, and on closer examination she noticed that it was a large tennis shoe, worn at the toe and positioned so that the lace was tucked beneath the heel. The social worker was able to confirm the facts regarding the hospital layout and later discovered the shoe on a window sill exactly as described by Maria. Many people have found the description of the shoe, particularly the accuracy of the minute details, to be very convincing.

Some people claim to have frequent out of body experiences independent of NDE. Dr Charles Tart, Professor of Psychology at the University of California, described a remarkable veridical out of body experience of a young woman whom he tested under laboratory conditions. The subject slept in a bed in the laboratory while under close observation. She had electrodes connected to her head to record brainwave patterns while she slept. The other ends of the electrode cables were connected to an electrode box at the head of the bed. There was enough slack wire to enable her to comfortably turn over in bed but not enough to allow her to sit up. After the subject had been connected to the equipment, Dr Tart placed a piece of paper, with five random numbers written on it, on a shelf which was situated over five feet above her head. The following morning, the subject was able to give Dr Tart the five digits in the correct sequence. She said she had left her body during the night, floated up towards the ceiling and read the numbers. The chances of guessing are 100,000 to one.

Both Maria's story and Dr Tart's experiment, and indeed all cases of veridical out of body experiences have weaknesses and have been explained away, admittedly not very convincingly by sceptics. A British psychiatrist, Dr Peter Fenwick, placed messages on ledges above eye level in the operating theatres of the hospital where he works. Patients floating up while going through OBE would be able to read the messages and relate them afterwards. No such reports have come from patients up to this point.

Efforts have been made to show that out of body experiences arise from purely physiological factors. Doctors in Switzerland discovered, while treating a patient for epilepsy, that it is possible to produce a floating, out of body experience by stimulating a particular part of the brain. The discovery was made quite accidentally. The patient had over 100 electrodes inserted in her brain in an effort to pinpoint the origin of seizures from which she had suffered for eleven years. Each time the electrode in a part of the brain known as the *angular gyrus* was stimulated, the woman felt that she was floating above her body and looking down upon herself. Doctors suggested that the angular gyrus plays an important part in synthesising visual information and the brain's touch and balance representation of the body. When the two types of data fail to coalesce and continue to exist separately, two separate perceptions of the body are created.

## A CONTINUING DEBATE

People who believe that a human being is a combination of mortal body and immortal soul find the reports of near-death and out of body experience very convincing, as they seem to validate belief in the dual nature of man. Those who believe that the mind cannot exist outside the body find the reports irritating and unsettling. The debate continues and neither side has yet produced a case strong enough to convince those occupying the middle ground.

The near-death experience seems to give credibility to some of the fundamental elements promoted for centuries by the major world religions, in particular the existence of a benign supreme being, and of an afterlife. Recurring themes in thousands of NDEs involve passing through a dark tunnel towards a bright light which resolves itself into a revered religious figure such as Jesus Christ. Reunions with deceased relatives and friends and glimpses of the landscape of paradise are common features in the NDEs of people of all cultures.

The sceptics argue that the NDE phenomenon is simply the subjective experience of the process of dying. Because it is a physiological process, the experience is the same for people of all cultures. The sensation of moving through a tunnel towards a bright light is produced by sudden discharges of nervous energy from the eyes and the visual receptors in the brain. Out of body experiences are powerful hallucinations, similar to those generated by certain kinds of drugs, and occur as the mind's integrity begins to break down. The point has also been made that a general belief in an afterlife may have arisen in ancient times from descriptions given by people who had had near-death experiences.

Many questions remain unanswered. Statistics based on a variety of studies show that between forty and eighty percent of patients who are clinically dead for a short period do not experience an NDE. If a near death experience is simply an hallucination generated by a disintegrating mind shortly before death, why does not every clinically dead person experience it? If an out of body experience could be fully validated, would it prove the existence of an afterlife? There is a rather large gap between accepting that consciousness can be physically separated from the body for a couple of minutes, on the one hand, and belief that the human psyche will continue to exist for all eternity, on the other.

Many religious people are not at all enthused by some of the reported NDEs. Far too many people seem to be headed for heaven. Even those who would be expected to be bound for the underworld, murderers, drug dealers, atheists, abortionists and the like, regularly report a very positive reception at the other side of the tunnel. Predictably, negative accounts of NDEs began to emerge, stories of people coming back to life in a state of absolute terror having been to hell for a few minutes.

US cardiologist Dr Maurice S. Rawlings brought much of this kind of material to public attention in two best selling books: *Beyond Death's Door* published in 1978 and, and a follow-up entitled *To Hell and Back* published in 1993. Dr Rawlings observed, first hand, some of his own patients undergoing terrifying NDEs. Many of them saw the tunnel of light turn into a ring of fire. One man described how the tunnel walls burst into flame and how he found himself near a huge burning lake. He saw a deceased friend being dragged round a corner and then heard his screams shortly afterwards. Another patient begged Dr Rawlings not to stop the CPR: 'don't stop, don't stop, I'm in hell! Don't you understand, every time you stop I'm in hell'. Dr Rawlings claims to have become a Christian after that particular experience. He wrote his books as cautionary tales.

Dr Rawlings also attempted to reinterpret the conventional NDE in order to account for the unacceptably large numbers that seemed to be going to heaven. He suggested that the departing souls were being deliberately deceived in an effort to lure them into hell. In many cases, he claimed, the light at the end of the tunnel was Satan. He also made the point that people unconsciously suppress negative experiences. Therefore, they often forgot the negative aspects of an NDE. He also contended that since he was in a position to interview patients immediately after their experience, the testimony he collected was more accurate than the data of other researchers. He estimated that the near-death experiences of about half of his patients were of the terrifying variety.

In both of his books, Dr Rawlings seems to be on a mission to frighten people into becoming followers of Jesus in order to avoid hell. The books have been criticised by renowned NDE expert Dr Michael Sabom who claims that distressing NDEs are very uncommon, regardless of the timing of the interview. Interestingly, none of the 62 patients in *The Lancet* study who had NDEs reported a distressing or frightening experience.

# 9. Death List

Each of the previous chapters examined an aspect of death and hopefully helped to fill in some gaps in your knowledge. What significance should be attributed to this information? That is entirely up to the reader. You can ignore the certainty of your own death and its implications for yourself and others. Indeed, denial is the default position on death in the Western World, as it is for death's accompaniments – sickness and old age. There are whole industries built round efforts to make the old appear young and, as we have seen, the dead appear alive.

'Nothing is certain but death and taxes', according to Benjamin Franklin. For tax returns, there is always a target date, a cut off point, well flagged in advance, with threats of fines and imprisonment to encourage you to take the appropriate actions before that date. Your deathday, the mother of all deadlines, may come at any time: like a thief in the night. The penalty for being unprepared for death applies less to the deceased than to those left behind. Many people leave a muddle behind them, and a grieving family poorly equipped to deal with it. People recognise that death is important, but only those who have been given a terminal diagnosis regard it as an urgent matter. Accordingly, 'prepare a death "to do" list' is never likely to appear in your annual schedule of new year's resolutions.

# *Debt List*

There are certain tasks that every conscientious person should carry out before death. Given that many of the items on the list are duties owed to those who will be left behind, perhaps 'debt list' would be a more suitable title for one's final 'to do' inventory. Not everyone gets a terminal prognosis. You could die suddenly and unexpectedly without any warning to yourself or your family. You could fade away, gradually losing your freedom and your marbles. A death list is important but not urgent. It can be done now or later. It can be postponed for ever, and it most cases it is. However, it makes sense to give attention to the following items while you are physically and mentally capable, rather than leaving them undone, or postponing them to a time when you will not be as well able to cope.

## 1. MAKE YOUR WILL

A will is a legal document detailing how you want to have your property disposed of after your death. As well as giving instructions regarding who is to inherit your goods, a will allows you to specify who is to administer your affairs This person is known as the executor – executrix if female – in legal parlance. A will is also the appropriate place in which to appoint legal guardians to care for your underage children; to indicate your funeral wishes; and to gift cash or specific items to particular persons. If you die without leaving a will, that is intestate, your property will be distributed according to the law of the jurisdiction in which you live. This may not be in accordance with your wishes.

Married couples tend to believe that if they die without making a will, the survivor will inherit the assets of the deceased partner. In many cases, this is not so. The absence of a will may result in unnecessary delay in the distribution of your property, the freezing of bank accounts, charges that could have been avoided, and inheritance tax that competent advice could have circumvented. A will also discourages disputes among beneficiaries, and deters disappointed people, who may have expected to benefit, from advancing claims.

It takes the law of the land some time to catch up with social change. Couples living together outside of marriage, those in same sex partnerships, separated people, and divorcees need to be particularly conscientious about making a will. Inheritance law may not recognise their existing partnerships and relationships and, in the absence of a will, may determine that their assets be distributed among the family of the deceased rather than given to a long standing existing partner.

You may need to change your will or, indeed, make several different wills, in the course of your lifetime, to take account of changes in your circumstances and changes in inheritance law. Nothing stands still for very long. For instance, while your children are still minors, it makes sense to appoint guardians in the event of your death. When they are of full age, guardians are no longer necessary, and you may at that stage wish to appoint your children as joint executors of your will. As time goes on, your assets may increase to a level at which your beneficiaries will have to pay tax on their inheritance. There are tax efficient ways of making wills which ensure that the minimum amount of tax is paid.

Composing a will requires the attention of a competent legal professional who is capable of drafting a document which takes into account your personal circumstances, your wishes, and the law of the land. The old English idiom, 'cut off with a shilling' refers to the belief that, in order to disinherit an heir, you had to bequeath him a small sum of money, such as a shilling. Otherwise, it would appear that he had been mistakenly overlooked and he could possibly manage to successfully contest the will. The law on inheritance can be still quite contrary. Appoint a professional to satisfy yourself that your will is written in the appropriate legal jargon that ensures your instructions are implemented after your death. Many internet sites offer a will writing service for a nominal sum of money. However, this may be false economy. Depending on your assets, it may also be wise to get the advice of a financial expert before finalising your will.

## 2. MAKE YOUR LIVING WILL

You cannot be given medical treatment without your consent, except under exceptional circumstances. However, if you are incapable of consenting due to unconsciousness or mental incapacity, you will receive whatever medical treatment the doctors consider to be in your best interests. Many people worry about the prospect of receiving medical treatment that is not in accordance with their wishes at a time when they are not in a position to object. To prevent this from happening you may specify in advance your medical care preferences so that these views may still be taken into account at a time when you are no longer able to articulate them. Such a statement is generally known as an 'advance directive'. It is also known as a 'living will', a 'health care declaration', an 'advance statement' or an 'advance refusal'.

Generally speaking, such instructions must be followed by doctors, provided that they are in conformity with certain principles. These principles include: not requesting the performance of any illegal act, such as euthanasia; and not demanding a specific type of treatment – this is the prerogative of your medical team. Essentially, an advance directive allows you to refuse rather than select treatments. In hospital, some procedures are indisputably for the patient's good, such as sanitary measures, including oral hygiene, and the administration of pain killers when required. Refusing such measures will not be entertained.

If you do not express your views, treatment to maintain your life by whatever means are available will be provided. This, of course, is something to be thankful for under normal circumstances. However, there are two sets of circumstances under which some people might not consider it to be desirable – in the case of terminal illness and in the case of permanent disability. Advance directives are often drawn up to cover these situations.

If you are suffering from a terminal illness, procedures which extend life may have a detrimental impact on quality of life. An advance directive could be used in this instance to opt for a shorter more comfortable life. Then, if you lose the power to communicate, your doctor is already aware of your views on treatment.

Drawing up an advance directive to cover how you would like to be treated in the event of your suffering from a serious and permanent disability is a much more difficult task. First of all, it is not possible to be sure whether a disability is permanent or reversible. Nothing is certain in medicine. Secondly, there is no general agreement on which types of disability are intolerable. You may find the aftermath of a stroke – dependency, reduced mobility, communication difficulties – to be unbearable, whereas others may be able to accept a more serious disability, such as the loss of higher mental functions brought about by dementia. For some, life in a persistent vegetative state – brought about, for instance, by oxygen deprivation during a coronary attack – is preferable to death.

It is not wise to draw up in advance a list of treatments you want to refuse, unless you know exactly what condition you are likely to be in when you are no longer able to communicate with your doctors. A ventilator, for example, can be used to prolong the life of a brain damaged patient, but it can also be an essential component in the recuperation of a coronary patient. By listing mechanically assisted breathing as a treatment you want to refuse, you could unwittingly condemn yourself to death in circumstances in which a full recovery is possible.

We have all heard of individuals who have been kept alive for decades by tube feeding while in a persistent vegetative state. The plight of such patients was addressed in 1990 by the US Supreme Court when it ruled that feeding tubes are a medical treatment never intended to keep someone alive indefinitely in an unconscious state. This cleared the way to allow the removal of feeding tubes from patients who were hopelessly unconscious and allowed them to die naturally. However, Pope John Paul II stated on 20 March 2004, at an international congress dealing with 'life-sustaining treatments and the vegetative state' that food and water, even if supplied artificially, are 'always' a natural means of preserving life, not a medical act. He said that hospitals and doctors are 'morally obligated' to continue artificial feeding for patients in a vegetative state. It is not quite clear yet what impact this pronouncement will have, though it is certain to make most doctors pause before taking the decision to discontinue tube feeding. This state of affairs should not stampede people into refusing this procedure in advance. It should be remembered that tube feeding is not used exclusively to sustain the lives of patients in a persistent vegetative state. It is routinely used for short periods on patients recovering from serious surgery.

The importance of drawing up an advance directive was underlined by the case of Terri Schiavo of St Petersburg, Florida. She collapsed in her home in 1990 at the age of 26 and suffered respiratory and cardiac arrest. She remained in a coma for ten weeks and was later diagnosed as being in a persistent vegetative state. In 1998 her husband and guardian Michael Schiavo petitioned the courts to remove her gastric feeding tube. Terri's parents, Robert and Mary Schindler, opposed this and seven years of litigation followed. By March 2005 fourteen appeals had been heard in the Florida courts and five more in the Federal Court. Her feeding tube had been removed and reinserted twice by court order. The courts continued to side with

Schiavo's husband, agreeing that she was in a persistent vegetative state, and would not want to be kept alive in that condition. Every legal avenue having been exhausted, her feeding tube was removed for the third and final time on 18 March 2005. She died thirteen days later at a Florida hospice aged 41. Had Terri Schiavo drawn up a clear statement of her medical treatment preferences, she might not be the subject of this cautionary tale.

An advance statement need not necessarily be a long and detailed document. The Alzheimer's Society has published a simple document, available on the internet, which may be personalised and adapted. In its basic form, it covers most of the concerns that people have about medical treatment during a period of serious disability or terminal illness. The essence of the statement is as follows:

'I declare that if at any time the following circumstances exist: that I suffer from one or more of the conditions listed in the schedule below; I have become unable to participate effectively in decisions about my medical care; and two independent doctors (one a consultant) are of the opinion that I am unlikely to recover from illness or impairment, then in those circumstances my directions are as follows: that I am not to be subjected to any medical intervention or treatment aimed at prolonging or sustaining my life; that any distressing symptoms (including any caused by lack of food and fluid) are to be fully controlled by appropriate analgesic or other treatment, even though that treatment may shorten my life.'

Five conditions appear on the 'schedule':

1. Alzheimer's disease or any other form of dementia
2. Severe and lasting brain damage due to injury, stroke, disease or other cause
3. Advanced degenerative disease of the nervous system (eg motor neurone disease)
4. Severe immune deficiency (eg Aids)
5. Advanced disseminated malignant disease (eg widespread lung cancer)

6. Any other condition of comparable gravity.

A 'do not resuscitate' (DNR) instruction is a form of advance directive. It is a request not to be subjected to cardiopulmonary resuscitation (CPR) if your heart or breathing stops. Incidentally, the instruction is known as a 'do not attempt resuscitation' (DNAR) in Britain – whether this is due to a more precise use of language or less confidence in the British medical profession is not clear. Some patients are unlikely to benefit from resuscitation, particularly those suffering from advanced cancer, kidney failure, severe infections such as pneumonia, and those who need a lot of help with their daily activities. Most patients who die in hospital have had a DNR order written for them. Without such an instruction, hospital staff would commence CPR on cardiac arrest. Outside of hospital, with so many people trained in CPR and the widespread availability of defibrillators, it may be more difficult to avoid CPR. An 85 year old retired nurse, Ms Frances Polack from Hampshire, tackled this problem by spending £25 on having a 'do not resuscitate' notice tattooed on her chest. Ms Polack is quoted as saying: 'I don't want to die twice. By resuscitating me, they would be bringing me back from the dead only for me to have to go through it again'.

The British Medical Association's guidelines on CPR make it clear that a DNAR drawn up by a patient must be taken into account, even if the doctors believe that the patient could be successfully resuscitated: '[Medical personnel] should refrain from artificially preserving life where it is clear that the patient would consider the resulting situation to be an "inhuman or degrading" state. The duty to protect life must be balanced with the obligation not to subject the patient to inhuman or degrading treatment'.

Another way of ensuring that your preferences regarding medical treatment are acted upon at a time when you are unable to communicate, is to appoint a health proxy. A durable power of attorney (DPA) for health care, names a person whom you have chosen to make health care decisions on your behalf. It becomes active any time you are unconscious or unable to make medical decisions. This may be a better option than an advance directive, provided there is someone you trust enough with this power. The appointment of a health proxy allows each new situation to be assessed as it occurs, making it unnecessary to lay down instructions for situations which may not happen in the way you may have predicted.

The legal position with regard to advance directives varies from one jurisdiction to another. However, even if the legal position is not clear, writing your preferences in advance ensures that those charged with your medical care are fully aware of your preferences. It also ensures that family members will not be fighting one another with regard to your treatment.

In the United States, state and federal court decisions have established the right of incompetent or comatose persons to have their wishes regarding medical treatment respected, provided those wishes are known. This recognition has given a sound legal basis to advance directives and doctors are obliged to abide by them, provided that they are drawn up in accordance with the principles already dealt with above.

In the United Kingdom advance directives are enforceable under common law. More specifically, under the Mental Capacity Act, section 24 – 'Advance decisions to refuse treatment' – gives advance directives the full backing of the law. The section confirms that people may make a decision in advance to refuse treatment if they should lose capacity in the future. However, some strict formalities must be complied with in order for the directive to be valid. In particular, the decision must be made in writing, signed and witnessed and in addition, there must be an express statement that the decision stands 'even if life is at risk'.

There is no legislation in relation to advance directives in

Ireland, so the legal position is not clear. A legal decision which may have some bearing on this area was made by the Supreme Court in July 1995. On that occasion four of the five judges consented to the discontinuation of the artificial feeding of a woman who had been in a persistent vegetative state for 23 years. The court considered that the withdrawal of life sustaining measures and the natural death that would follow, was in the best interests of the patient as there was no prospect of improvement. The judges, however, did not lay down any overall guidelines as to how similar cases might be determined.

Prior to the Supreme Court decision, the case had come before the High Court where Judge Lynch took the opportunity of summarising Irish medical practice in the treatment of terminally ill patients at that time, and of accepting that such practices were lawful. He said that a competent terminally ill patient is entitled to demand that life support systems be either withdrawn or not provided. In the case of incompetent terminally ill patients, the carers, in agreement with the patient's representatives such as family or friends, may withdraw or refrain from providing life support systems, if they believe it to be in the best interests of the patient. If, in such a case, the representatives of the patient are not in agreement with a decision by the carers to withdraw life support measures, a second medical opinion is sought. The second medical opinion determines how the patient is to be treated. In the case of an incompetent patient, whether terminally ill or not, where the patient's representatives believe that life support should be withdrawn and the carers disagree, the life maintaining measures should be left in place unless and until a High Court order to the contrary is obtained by the patient's representatives.

No significant statements which have a clear bearing on the legal force of an advance directive have been made by the Irish judiciary since then. Neither has any relevant legislation been passed. In 2003 the Law Reform Commission made a brief statement on the matter: 'The Commission considers that it is unnecessary to embark on a detailed analysis of these complex issues. Advance care directives and their affects may be considered more comprehensively in a future paper'.

However, given the crystal clear right a person has under Irish law to refuse medical treatment in almost all situations, doctors who choose to ignore an advance directive put themselves in danger of civil and criminal prosecution. Supreme Court Justice Denham set forth the right to refuse treatment as follows:

'Medical treatment may not be given to an adult person of full capacity without his or her consent. There are a few rare exceptions to this e.g. in regard to contagious diseases or in a medical emergency where the patient is unable to communicate. This right arises out of civil, criminal and constitutional law. If medical treatment is given without consent it may be a trespass against the person in civil law, or battery in criminal law and a breach of the individual's constitutional rights. The consent which is given by an adult of full capacity is a matter of choice. It is not necessarily a decision based on medical consideration. Thus, medical treatment may be refused for other than medical reasons. Such reasons may not be viewed as good medical reasons, or reasons most citizens would regard as rational, but a person of full age capacity may make decisions for their own reasons'.

An Irish High Court decision since then may give some grounds for concern regarding the right to refuse medical treatment. In September 2006, Justice Henry Abbott ruled in favour of the Coombe maternity hospital which had requested permission to subject a patient to a blood transfusion against her will. The 23 year old Congolese national had lost most of her blood due to a haemorrhage after giving birth to a son, and was in imminent danger of death. As a Jehovah's Witness she considered taking blood in any form to be against the laws of God. The judge decided in favour of the transfusion because the baby would, apparently, have nobody to look after him in Ireland in the event of his mother's death. However, it is difficult to imagine how Justice Abbott's doctrine could be applied beyond the narrow circumstances of that particular case.

## 3. DECIDE ON ORGAN DONATION

Organ donation has already been discussed. It is only likely to become an issue if you end up in an intensive care unit attached to a ventilator suffering from very serious brain injuries. Then, if you are diagnosed as being brain dead, your family may be asked whether they are willing to give permission for the removal of your organs for transplantation purposes. The great benefits which would accrue to the organ recipients will be alluded to by the hospital staff in an effort to get a positive response and your family will be faced with a very difficult decision. It is unlikely that they will be in a position to give the matter as much consideration as it deserves at such a difficult time. Therefore, it makes sense to come to a decision yourself while you are in the full of your health. You may not feel comfortable with the prospect of having your organs removed while your heart is still beating; you may have difficulty accepting the concept of brain death; you may find the notion of taking life saving organs to the grave with you as selfish. Whatever your views, your decision should be related to your family so that they may represent your wishes if it ever becomes necessary.

It is becoming more important than ever to have your views on organ donation clearly stated. There are two systems in operation regarding obtaining permission to remove the organs of a brain dead patient. The 'opt-in' system operates in Ireland, the UK and the USA. It requires the prior consent of the patient — in the form of a donor's card — or the patient's relatives, before organs or tissues may be removed. The 'opt-out' system assumes that all citizens consent to donation unless they have specifically expressed a wish to the contrary.

The European Commission is currently considering the question of a directive in respect of organ transplantation, including the issue of consent, and proposes to conduct a thorough scientific evaluation of the situation. It will present a report on its analysis to the Council of the European Union. The findings of this report will certainly influence the legislation on organ donation of all the EU member countries. There appears to be a strong and growing lobby in favour of the opt-out system. In September 2005, the Irish Council for Bioethics conducted a survey in which a cross section of Irish people were asked to express their level of agreement or disagreement with the statement: 'Consent to organ donation should be assumed unless the person expressly states otherwise, in an effort to increase organ donation'. The results indicated an even split on the issue.

In April 2006, during Organ Donor Awareness Week, Deputy Brian O'Shea lobbied the Minister for Health to implement measures that would improve the supply of organs available for transplantation. His statement, quoted in the press, appeared to endorse the idea that everyone should be assumed to be an organ donor. He also expressed concern that a patient's previously expressed willingness to become an organ donor could be overruled by the patient's family. In Britain, under the provisions of the Human Tissue Act, bereaved families have lost their right to veto the wishes of a family member who expressed a clear desire to donate organs for transplantation purposes after death.

The bottom line with regard to organ donation seems to be, if you do not want your organs to be removed after being pronounced brain dead, you had better put your views in writing and inform your family of your decision.

4. RECORD YOUR FAMILY HISTORY
'Who's that person over there?' is a question that's often heard in all sorts of social situations. The response elicited tends to be a description of the one deed that defines the person in question,

rather than a brief biography: he's the one who was put off the road for drunken driving, or rescued a woman from a burning building, or won the lottery, or fought in Iraq, and so on.

Some people's fame spreads beyond local folk memory and they become the subject of media reports after death. Welsh sports star Ken Jones died in April 2006. He was a sports celebrity, well known for having been an international rugby star and an Olympic silver medallist. These facts were mentioned briefly in the first three lines of his obituary. The remaining 20 lines related this story: '…in 1958 he carried the Queen's speech in a baton into the stadium for the opening of the Commonwealth Games in Cardiff. The previous runner failed to reach the stadium entrance by the time Prince Philip was ready to receive the speech, so officials thrust a new baton – with the speech inside – into Jones' hand and told him to run. Flustered by the crisis and blinded by the sun, he ran the wrong way round the stadium, taking much longer than scheduled. Then he mistook the lord lieutenant of Glamorgan – resplendent in military uniform – for Prince Philip, who was wearing a suit.' When a choice has to be made between respect and entertainment, the media will always opt for the latter, even in a genre as solemn as an obituary.

How will you be remembered? Unless you write down a few facts about yourself before you die, you are unlikely to be remembered at all. Most people know nothing about any forebear further back than their grandparents – not even a name. People generally do not expect to be forgotten so soon. Certainly, the data recorded about you by state agencies is likely to be round for quite a while, but facts like the amount of income tax you paid hardly qualifies as biographical information.

This situation is easily rectified: write, for your descendants, a short account of your life and times. Include in it a detailed account of your family, adding information about your brothers,

FIGURE 10: THE IMPORTANCE OF RECORDING THE OBVIOUS: TIME
TRANSFORMS THE HUMBLEST GENEALOGICAL WRITINGS INTO HOLY
WRIT AND THE HUMBLEST SCRIBES INTO FAMILY PATRIARCHS...

sisters, parents, grandparents; going back to earlier generations
if you are able. Family history is one of the most popular hob-
bies in the world. The greatest sources of genealogical information are the living. What can be recalled and recorded effort-
lessly by individuals about their family background is literally
beyond price. Certainly, a professional genealogist could be
hired, at a hefty hourly rate, and could probably locate basic
birth, marriage and death information in various archives, but a
researcher could never access the stories and anecdotes that put
life into a family tree. Only the living can give this information.
You might feel a little foolish to be writing down the obvious,
what everyone seems to know, but in thirty, sixty, or a hundred
years time, the information that seems so trite at the time of
writing will be regarded as genealogical gold by the yet unborn.

The importance of recording the obvious is crucial, and easily demonstrated by considering the type of family history materials that are passed down from earlier generations. Very many

families have collections of old sepia photographs, hidden away in attics, stuffed into drawers, and in shoeboxes under the bed. Their place of origin is often unknown. The long dead, in military uniforms or costumes of a bygone age, stare out: unknown faces. The connection has been lost because most of the photographs are without names or, indeed, captions of any kind.

As the decades roll by after your death, your family history statement will increase in importance. What seemed to be banal when it was first written will by then have become venerable to new generations. It will be reproduced and sent to other branches of the family. Imagine how highly valued would be a document penned in 1750 by one of your ancestors, giving a description of family life and times two and a half centuries ago. That kind of time span transforms the humblest genealogical writings into holy writ, and the humblest scribes into family patriarchs and matriarchs.

## 5.PLAN YOUR FUNERAL

Plan your own funeral! You might regard this notion with the same revulsion as the idea of digging your own grave, but you must remember that, if you don't plan it, somebody else must. It makes matters much easier for your family if you, at least, make a few key decisions. Chief among these are whether you wish to be embalmed, and whether you would prefer burial or cremation. Selecting a coffin is also important as it is the most expensive item associated with a funeral. These matters were discussed in detail in Chapter 6: 'It's Your Funeral'.

Funeral rituals aim to provide a dignified parting by the living from the dead. Modern practice emphasises the importance of viewing the deceased. If you decide against embalming, you are almost certainly opting for a closed coffin, that is, no viewing of the body. Undertakers are very reluctant to allow an open coffin unless the body has been embalmed, justifiably claiming that without this procedure, unmistakable signs of decomposition may suddenly become apparent, causing unnecessary distress. An unembalmed body, according to undertakers, may also constitute a health hazard. Embalming is a highly invasive process, draining the blood and filling the circulatory system with toxic chemicals. The preservative properties of formaldehyde also greatly retard the natural decomposition of the body in the grave, whereas most people would probably prefer to return to dust as soon as possible.

On the positive side, the use of a pink dye in embalming fluid gives an embalmed body a much more lifelike colour, and the services of a skilful mortician can give a natural, relaxed look to the face. Some people might object to the undertaker being given free rein to treat a body as a canvas on which to practise his cosmetic arts, stitching, stuffing, gluing, dyeing and painting the corpse back to a counterfeit of life. They might argue that a body should be allowed to retain something of the integrity of death to help the mourners to understand the imperative of a final parting. There is a counter argument. Many people are worn out by illness or disfigured in accidents. It is very consoling for family and friends to see loved ones restored for the last time to their former appearance. The final viewing, then, can cancel out the memories of suffering on a deathbed and leave an image of the deceased which brings happier times to mind. After all, the body is going to be buried or burned, and people are not averse to enhancing their appearance in life by the use of cosmetics and other measures.

Most people opt for embalming, believing that it is important for family and friends to have one last look at the deceased. If youare implacably opposed to embalming, it may be possible to arrange a short period for family and friends to view the body immediately after death, either in the hospital ward or mortuary, or in the home. Others may be given the opportunity of paying their respects in a funeral home or church with the coffin closed with, perhaps, a framed photograph of the deceased on display.

A final point about embalming worth mentioning is that, in Ireland in particular, the procedure seems to be routinely carried out unless the person making the funeral arrangements requests that it should not be done: it's an opt out situation. Does this suggests a kind of conspiracy of silence between the undertaker and the customer? The undertaker does not want to explain the procedure and the customer does not want to know?

With regard to body disposal, generally, cremation costs less than burial. It is quick, clean, modern and, as a way to go, is inexorably overtaking burial. It has a number of drawbacks, however. While you never have to travel very far to a cemetery, in many jurisdictions the nearest crematorium may be hundreds of miles away. Consequently, the body usually has to be sent away to be cremated. The process itself takes twenty-four hours or more. The absence of the corpse for a day or two and its return in the form of 'cremains', does not fit in very well with traditional funeral rituals. In the case of a funeral involving burial, the mourners are in the continuous presence of the deceased from the beginning of the ceremony up to the filling of the grave. This helps to bring closure, in a literal and psychological sense, to the calamity of death.

The coffin is the most expensive item associated with a funeral. It is a well known phenomenon that the bereaved who have to choose a coffin for a loved one, normally opt for neither the cheapest nor the dearest, but for one in the middle. Since people generally have no idea what a coffin costs, an undertaker not averse to sharp practice may pick the range of coffins to be shown to customers very carefully and with an eye to his own profit. In the United States, undertakers are required by law to draw attention to the availability of an unfinished wood box or alternative container for direct cremation. In the rest of the world, there are no such restrictions.

You could select your own coffin. Many undertakers offer the choice of paying for your funeral in advance. This arrangement allows 'customers' to review everything at a time when death is not a pressing problem and it removes entirely the burden of the funeral from the family.

If the rest of the developed world follow the lead of the United States, the traditional coffin will eventually be replaced by the casket style coffin. Then, selecting the type of receptacle to be buried in will become much more difficult. A casket is usually chosen on the basis of two characteristics which are regarded as important. First of all, its appearance. Apart from the corpse, the casket is the principal item on display at the viewing and the main focus of attention at the church ceremony and at the committal afterwards in the graveyard. Its quality and appearance are undoubtedly noticed by the mourners. It may be seen as reflecting the calibre and social standing of the deceased. If the body is to be cremated, it may not be regarded as a status symbol to the same extent.

Secondly, strength and durability seem to be regarded as highly desirable casket qualities, and these features are usually highlighted in manufacturers' advertisements. Why people should wish to have their bodies indefinitely preserved is unclear, but the same desire is reflected in other practices originating in the United States, such as embalming, the use of grave liners, and the popularity of vaults, some of them steel enforced to make them earthquake proof. The cult of preservation can have little to do with a literal belief in the resurrection because it is hard to see how people can be expected to come back to life with formaldehyde instead of blood in their veins.

Archaeologists of the future are the only ones likely to benefit from modern American burial practices. Rameses the Great, who ruled Egypt during the time of Moses, did not expect to end up in a glass case in the Cairo Museum. Thousands of Egyptian mummies were sold to tourists in the nineteenth century and brought back as souvenirs to Europe and America where many had their winding cloths removed as a form of sophisticated entertainment at 'unwrapping' parties. In a few thousand years time American funeral paraphernalia, bones and all, may have become prized collectors' items in a new geo-political world.

A religious affiliation will normally help to determine many of the details of an adherent's funeral. The relevant clergyman, when contacted, will liaise with the undertaker, slot in the funeral services to a mutually agreeable time and discuss the details of the ceremony with the family. At that stage the readings from favourite passages of scripture may be requested, or this may be left up to the expertise of the clergyman.

Many people find the funeral rituals of the various Christian denominations to be rather impersonal, and it has become quite common for a friend or relative to speak some words about the deceased at the end of the ceremony. Whoever is to give the funeral oration, if that is not too pompous a term for it, should be asked well in advance, and the clergyman should be informed so that he can call upon the speaker at the appropriate time.

## 6. PLAN YOUR DEATHBED SCENE

Writers of fiction, especially dramatists, have always put huge creative energy into devising death bed scenes. Before an important character shuffles off this mortal coil, something really impressive is anticipated: reconciliation, confession, divulging of secrets, philosophical insights, witty last words, or some other kind of moving performance. Since most people have rarely if ever witnessed a real death bed scene, the template provided by the greatest writers in the world is their only guide.

Thankfully, real life is not usually like that. A dying person is not expected to have the energy or inclination for turning in an Oscar winning performance. For the family and friends, attendance at a deathbed alternates between stress and boredom. This is well captured in one of Emily Dickinson's poems in which the solemn mourners round a deathbed waiting for the loved one to pass away are totally distracted by the most trivial thing imaginable – the buzzing of a fly. It must be unnerving for many patients to see long faced relatives sitting round the bed, waiting for…

Perhaps the most important factor during the last days and hours of a person's life is for someone to take complete charge of the situation: to ensure that the patient's advance directive is fully respected, to control the flow of visitors and to carry out whatever instructions the dying person may have given.

## 7. DEATHBED CONVERSION?

Many people put off formulating their thoughts on God and religion until they are terminally ill. At that point, fear of eternal damnation may act as a strong antidote to scepticism. Arguments in support of various religious doctrines, previously perceived as weak, may now appear to have greater potency. Though there is only one instance of a deathbed conversion in the *Bible*, it affirms for the believer, in the clearest terms possible, the power of a last minute change of heart. The passage, relating the story of the good thief who was crucified with Jesus Christ, is to be found in *Luke* (23:39-43): 'One of the criminals who hung there hurled insults at him: "Aren't you the Christ? Save yourself and us!" But the other criminal rebuked him. "Don't you fear God", he said, "since you are under the same sentence? We are punished justly, for we are getting what our deeds deserve. But this man has done nothing wrong". Then he said, "Jesus, remember me when you come into your kingdom". Jesus answered him, "I tell you the truth, today you will be with me in paradise".'

It has been suggested that a greater openness to matters spiritual among the terminally ill may be nothing more than a manifestation of 'Pascal's Wager'. According to Blaise Pascal, a seventeenth century French philosopher, mathematician and inventor, regardless of any evidence for or against the existence of God, failure to accept God's existence risks losing everything with no payoff, so the best bet is to accept the existence of God. The argument goes something like this: if you believe in God and God does not exist, you lose nothing because death ends all; if you believe in God and God exists, you gain an eternity in Heaven; if you disbelieve in God and God does not exist, you gain nothingas death is the end of all; however, if you disbelieve in God and God actually exists, you lose everything as you will suffer eternal damnation. Therefore, it is rational to believe in God.

There have been several counter-arguments to the Pascal's Wager. One clear objection is that belief is not a matter of choice: you cannot will yourself to believe in something that appears to be false. Following on from that, a just God is hardly likely to reward dishonesty. There is also the problem of the multiplicity of gods. Back the wrong god and you put yourself in the same position as the unbeliever. Passages may be quoted from the *Bible* indicating that non-belief in the divinity of Jesus Christ and in the Holy Trinity will result in damnation. Muslims, who believe in neither, can quote the *Koran* which promises damnation to those who do not believe in the indivisible Allah, which Christians reject. Theological debate is hardly an area for a terminally ill person to get involved in. Benjamin Franklin summed up the nature of theological disputes as: 'Many a long dispute among divines may be thus abridged: It is so. It is not so. It is so. It is not so'.

There are many stories of deathbed conversions. Even the most unlikely candidates, we are asked to believe, recant and embrace orthodoxy at the end of their days. Thomas Paine was the author of *The Rights of Man*, and one of the fathers of the American Revolution. Later in life he wrote *The Age of Reason* in which he rejected the *Bible* as the word of God in the most trenchant terms. He mercilessly applies his brand of reason and scepticism to every part of sacred scripture. In one instance he refers to the Israelites, sanctioned by God, coming by stealth upon whole nations of people – who had given them no offence – and putting them to the sword, sparing neither age nor infancy, and suggests that to believe the *Bible* to be true, we must unbelieve all our belief in the moral justice of God 'for wherein could crying or smiling infants offend?'. His attacks on Christianity lost him most of his friends and only six people attended his funeral. Soon after his death, stories of his deathbed conversion were being taught at Sunday school. Of course, Paine never changed his views, despite at least four separate efforts to get him to accept the divinity of Jesus while he was on his death bed.

Charles Darwin is regarded as one of the greatest scientists of all time, on a par with Aristotle, Galileo and Newton. His theory of evolution – which contradicted the *Book of Genesis* – and his profession of agnosticism, established him as the premier symbol of rational thought. Therefore, the story of his conversion to Christianity and his renunciation of the theory of evolution during his last illness, created a sensation, when it was first published in August 1915. The story was recounted by Lady Hope who said that she had called on the great scientist shortly before his death, and in the course of a conversation with her, he seemed greatly distressed, 'his fingers twitched nervously, and a look of agony came over his face as he said: "I was a young man with unformed ideas. I threw out queries, suggestions, wondering all the time over everything, and to my astonishment, the ideas took like wildfire. People made a religion of them".' He then requested Lady Hope to arrange a religious service in a summer house in the garden the following day and said that he would keep the window of his bedroom open and join in the singing of hymns. All of Darwin's family rejected Lady Hope's story. His daughter Henrietta had this to say: 'I was present at his deathbed...He never recanted any of his scientific views, either then or earlier. We think the story of his conversion was fabricated in the USA . . . '

The great North American Indian chief, Crazy Horse, is quoted as saying: 'Today would be a good day to die, while I still have all the important things in my life round me'. If you do not die while in your prime, you could always cast your mind back and try to recall what you believed then when you were at the peak of your intellectual powers. You might decide to hold fast to those views rather than modifying them at a time when your mental powers are weakened. However, there is always a counter view. Some people believe in God only when they are driving at 100 miles per hour, or standing on the top rung of a ladder or after a death sentence has been pronounced on them by a judge or a doctor. The Christian churches have always stressed the redemptive powers of suffering, suggesting that it opens human perception to a spiritual world, hidden from the smug and comfortable. Terminal illness, therefore, could be regarded as a time of epiphany; a unique opportunity to progress spiritually.

It is ironic that the best advice in this area comes from the bumbling fool, Polonius, in Shakespeare's play *Hamlet*:

'To thine own self be true and,
And it must follow, as the night the day,
Thou canst not then be false to any man.'

Or indeed, any God!

# 10. Last Words

Though the last words spoken by any human being have a curiosity value, they must have some special merit to be noted and quoted. The final phrases of the famous are an exception to the rule. Even if they are bland and vacuous the celebrity value of the speaker endows them with significance. Bing Crosby collapsed and died after playing a round of golf in 1977; his last words are still well known, despite their triteness: 'It was a great game'. Even last words which consist of no more than rambling phrases such as: 'France, the Army, head of the Army, Josephine', are likely to be immortalised, if they were spoken by someone of great importance like – as in this case – Napoleon Bonaparte. Consequently, you can expect any collection of last words to be quite variable in quality.

Some people never quite get round to speaking last words. Ironically, two people who often feature in anthologies of last words, fit into this category. Calvin Coolidge, the thirtieth President of the United States, was a man of few words. On one occasion, during a White House dinner, a guest told the President that she had wagered that she could get him to speak at least three words in the course of the meal. His only response was: 'You lose'. Not unexpectedly, no last words are recorded for 'Silent Cal'. Dorothy Parker, the American writer and humorist filled the vacuum with a phrase that ever is associated ever since with that president's passing. When she was told that Coolidge was dead, she asked: 'How could they tell?' The Mexican rebel leader Pancho Villa was assassinated in 1923. Reporters managed to gain access to him while he was dying and requested his last words. He was unable to think of anything appropriate to say and felt diminished by his lack of inspiration. He finally said: 'Don't let it end like this. Tell them I said something'.

Worse than being caught for words, perhaps, is to come out with the wrong words on your death bed. When King George V was dying, his doctor, in an effort to cheer him up, said: 'your majesty will soon be able to visit Bognor' – a resort town in West Sussex which had been renamed 'Bognor Regis' in the king's honour after his visit in 1929. The king's response, also his last words, was: 'Bugger Bognor'. However, *The London Times* fabricated last words more appropriate to a man of his elevated station: 'How is the Empire?'

FIGURE 11: KING GEORGE V: HIS LAST WORDS WERE 'BUGGER BOGNOR', THOUGH THE *LONDON TIMES* REPORTED THAT HE USED HIS LAST BREATH TO ENQUIRE: 'HOW IS THE EMPIRE'.

Some last words are startling because they are so contrary to expectations. At the time of his death in 1885, William Vanderbilt was acknowledged as the richest man in the world; his wealth was estimated at $200 million dollars. With his last breath he seems to have tried to elicit sympathy because he did not get the full measure of satisfaction from his great wealth: 'I have had no real gratification or enjoyment of any sort more than my neighbour on the next block who is worth only half a million'.

When death comes out of the blue, the last words spoken must suffice as last words. Sometimes they turn out to be very ironic. Hollywood actor Douglas Fairbanks Snr, in reply to a servant's enquiry regarding his health, said: 'Never felt better'. He died later that day. General John Sedgwick was the most senior army officer killed on either side during the American Civil War. However, he is best known for his last words, which were spoken at the beginning of the battle of Spotsylvania in 1864. While remonstrating with his men for taking cover from Confederate sharpshooters who were more than 1,000 yards away, he was killed by a bullet which struck him below his left eye. He had just spoken the words: 'They couldn't hit an elephant at this distance'.

Archduke Franz Ferdinand and his wife were assassinated by Gavrilo Princip in August 1914. His last words, referring to his fatal wound, were: 'It is nothing. It is nothing'. However, the death of the royal couple sparked off World War I, which resulted in the deaths of more than 10 million people.

Some people stay focussed on their business right to the end. When Conrad N. Hilton, founder of the Hilton Hotel chain, was asked on his deathbed for some words of wisdom, he said: 'Leave the shower curtain on the inside of the tub'. Nostradamus, the sixteenth century prophet who is credited with predicting most of the great events in history, including World War I, the rise of Adolf Hitler and World War II, seems to have practiced his trade to the very end. Asked for a comment when he was close to death, he said: 'Tomorrow I shall no longer be here'.

The last words of philosophers are usually awaited with eager anticipation, in the hope that something of great significance will be said. German philosopher Georg Wilhelm Hegel was regarded as one of the great minds of the nineteenth century, but his last words turned out to be as inscrutable as much of his philosophical writings: 'Only one man ever understood me. And he really didn't understand me'. His fellow countryman, Karl Marx, was equally disappointing on his deathbed. Asked by his housekeeper whether he had anything to say before he died – she undertook to write down whatever he wished to say – his response was: 'Go on, get out! Last words are for fools who haven't said enough'. The English philosopher Thomas Hobbes' last words suggest that after a lifetime of thinking he was no wiser than anyone else on the subject of death: 'It is my turn to take a leap into the darkness'. Voltaire, philosopher of the French enlightenment, was more spirited at the end. When asked on his deathbed to forswear Satan he said: 'This is no time to make new enemies.' He is also reported to have said, when a candle flared up while he was dying: 'What? Flames already!'

Even more is expected of writers and artists, but they do not always deliver. John Field, the great nineteenth century Irish pianist and composer was asked on his deathbed whether he was a Papist or a Calvinist. He may have misunderstood the question because his response was: 'I am a pianist'. Jane Austen's last words were in reply to her sister who asked if there was anything she wanted: 'Nothing but death'. Brendan Behan, the irreverent, hell raising Irish playwright spoke his last words to a nun who nursed him in hospital: 'Bless you, Sister. May all your sons be bishops'. Dylan Thomas' last words turned out to be a statement of cause of death: 'I've had eighteen straight whiskies, I think that's the record'. Oscar Wilde was famous for his witticisms and his last words have been variously reported as: 'My wallpaper and I are fighting a duel to the death. One or other of us has got to go'; and: 'I am dying beyond my means'.

It is difficult to avoid the suspicion that Wilde's last words were contrived by someone familiar with the writer's style. Many of the purported last words of revolutionaries and saints suggest they were the invention of those who belong to the same cause. The third century Christian martyr, St Lawrence, was condemned by the Roman authorities to be roasted alive on a gridiron. He faced his fate with unconcern, remarking to his executioners shortly before he died: 'See, I am done enough on one side, now turn me over and cook the other'.

Some great minds just don't put in the effort at the end. Richard Feynman was a teacher, scientist and musician; he helped to develop the atomic bomb, was a Nobel Prizewinning physicist and pioneer of nanotechnology. He contracted cancer in the mid-1980s. Eventually, he decided to discontinue treatment and died in February 1988. He once remarked: 'I don't *have* to know an answer. I don't feel frightened by not knowing things, by being lost in the mysterious universe without having any purpose – which is the way it really is, as far as I can tell, possibly. It doesn't frighten me'. What an excellent deathbed statement this would have made. His actual last words, however, were much more mundane: 'I'd hate to die twice, it's so boring'. The last words spoken by the great British statesman Winston Churchill, also a Nobel prizewinner, mirrored those of Feynman: 'I'm bored with it all'.

People who commit suicide have time to work on their final words. George Eastman founded the Eastman Kodak company and invented roll film which far surpassed photographic plates and, revolutionised photography. At the age of 77, having contracted a painful spinal disease, he put his affairs in order and killed himself with a pistol shot to the heart. His suicide note read: 'My work is done, why wait?' The last words of

Lawrence Oates, spoken on the day of his thirty-second birth-day, were: 'I am just going out and I may be some time'. He was part of the 1912 South Pole expedition lead by 'Scott of the Antarctic'. After suffering severe frostbite he felt he was a bur-den to the others and stepped out of the tent into a severe bliz-zard and certain death.

Those awaiting execution also have time to ponder on their last words. The famous Australian outlaw Ned Kelly, executed in 1880, contented himself with a cliché: 'Such is life'. James French was executed in the electric chair in 1966. He opted for a pun. Before his death he said to journalists: 'How about this for a headline in tomorrow's paper? "French fries"'.

The best of the 'last words' genre consist of statements which not only epitomise the speaker, but allow him to manifest his true nature for the last time. Two of the most outstanding exam-ples were spoken during the French Revolution by people who took opposite sides.

Thomas de Mahay, Marquis de Favras was arrested during the French Revolution and accused of helping King Louis XVI in his efforts to escape from France. In 1790, the nobleman was found guilty and sentenced to death. Before being led to the gal-lows to be hanged – the guillotine had not yet been commis-sioned – the clerk who had written out the death sentence hand-ed the document to the Marquis. He read over it. Then, in a sin-gle sentence, he managed to show his contempt for the people, the haughtiness of a French aristocrat, and courage in facing execution. Addressing the clerk he said: 'I see that you have made three spelling mistakes'.

George Jaques Danton was one of the leaders of the Revolution. He was a talented public speaker, combining a great delivery with a very telling turn of phrase. Tall and mus-cular with a large head, he had a resounding voice and was known variously, by friends and enemies alike, as a Titan, 'Jove the Thunderer', and the 'rebel Satan'. When he was a child he had been kicked in the face by a bull, and the scarring added to his singular appearance. He became first president of the Committee of Public Safety, a body of six men, who were entrusted with absolute executive power. Danton's committee began the Reign of Terror, sending thousands of people to the guillotine. However, having been overthrown by his arch rival Maximilien Robespierre, he was soon facing public execution himself. On his way to the guillotine he was downcast and sentimental at first, thinking of his wife and family, then Danton cast off that weak demeanour and took on again the fiery spirit of his earlier days. His last words were to Sanson his executioner: 'Show my head to the people. It's worth seeing'.

The 'foremost man in all the world', Gaius Julius Caesar, was assassinated at the Roman forum on 15 March – the ides of March – 44 BC. A military genius, a consummate politician and an outstanding writer, Caesar has always been regarded as one of the greatest human beings of all time. Among the conspirators who murdered him was Marcus Junius Brutus, a man whom Caesar had trusted and treated like a son. Roman historians describe Caesar as resisting the assassins until he saw Brutus raise his dagger against him. Then he put up no further fight. He covered up his face in his tunic and died at the base of Pompey's statue. The savage onslaught left 35 stab wounds on his body. Caesar's last words were 'Et tu, Brute?' – you also Brutus? Caesar's succinct charge of ingratitude against Brutus was afterwards taken up by Mark Antony, who used it to turn the Roman mob against Brutus and his co-conspirators. The assassins wanted to cast themselves in the role of patriots, men so concerned about the impact of Caesar's imperial ambitions on freedom, that they had to kill him. Caesar's dying phrase tainted them with treachery. His great facility with language and a lifetime of thinking three steps ahead of everyone else, enabled Caesar to give his supporters, with his dying breath, a powerful weapon in the struggle that was to follow. Far beyond the boundaries of the Roman Empire, two thousand years after the event, Caesar's last words still form part of our general knowledge. The words live on, even though the language they were spoken in has died out.

Caesar's last words were outshone by those of another man, who was born within the Roman Empire 44 years after Caesar's death. For many Christians, the dying words of Jesus Christ express the most appropriate deathbed attitude. There may be some objection, however, to including the words of Jesus on the cross in this 'last words' section. Christians believe that Jesus arose from the dead three days after the crucifixion, and remained on earth preaching the gospel for a further 40 days, before ascending into heaven from Mount Olivet. There are three accounts of the ascension in the *Bible*. They are quite similar in that in each one, Jesus is described as giving instructions to his apostles before leaving them; but the last words attributed to Jesus are quite different in each of the descriptions. In Mark's gospel he refers to the signs that will accompany those who believe in him, finishing with: '..they will lay their hands on the sick, and they will recover'. In Luke's gospel he says: 'And behold, I send the promise of my Father upon you; but stay in the city, until you are clothed with power from on high'. The third description is in the *Acts of the Apostles* and Jesus says: '…you shall receive power when the Holy Spirit has come upon you; and you shall be my witnesses in Jerusalem and in all Judea and Samaria and to the end of the earth.'

Christians repeat on their deathbed the last words of Jesus on the cross – which were not his last words – in the hope that their last words may not be their last words either:

'Father, into thy hands I commend my spirit'.


## END

# Select Bibliography

Bass, Bill & Jon Jefferson: *Death's Acre: inside the legendary body farm*, New York, 2003

Bondeson, Jan: *Buried Alive: the terrifying history of our most primal fear*, New York, 2002

De Quincey, Thomas: *Confessions of an English Opium Eater*, London, 1821

Drexler, K. Eric: *Engines of Creation: the coming era of nanotechnology*, New York, 1986

Ettinger, Robert: *The Prospect of Immortality,* New York, 1964

Kubler-Ross, Elisabeth: *On Death and Dying,* New York, 1969

Levine, Stephen: *Who Dies?*, New York, 1982

Moody, Raymond A.: *Life after Life: the investigation of a phenomenon – survival of bodily death*, New York, 1975

Rawlings, Maurice S.: *Beyond Death's Door*, New York, 1978

Rawlings, Maurice S.: *To Hell and Back,* New York, 1993